ATM

The Key to High-Speed Broadband Networking

ATM

The Key to High-Speed Broadband Networking

I.J. "Duffy" Hines

M&T Books
A Division of MIS:Press, Inc.
A Subsidiary of Henry Holt and Company, Inc.
115 West 18th Street
New York, New York 10011

Library of Congress Cataloging-in-Publication Data

Hines, I.J.
   ATM / I.J. "Duffy" Hines.
    p.   cm.
   ISBN 1-55851-443-0
   1. Asynchronous transer mode. I. Title.
   TK5105.35.H56   1996
   004.6'6—dc20   96-15270
                                                              CIP

10 9 8 7 6 5 4 3 2 1

Associate Publisher: *Paul Farrell*

Managing Editor: *Cary Sullivan*   **Production Editor:** *Anne Incao*
Development Editor: *Jono Hardjowirogo*   **Technical Editor:** *Greg Nunemacher*
Copy Edit Manager: *Shari Chappell*   **Copy Editor:** *Thomas Crofts*

Dedication

To my wife and children:

Sheryl—for your support and encouragement

Doni, I.J., and Tina—for your consideration,
cooperation, and assistance

To Mother, and all my brothers, sisters

In memory of Phoebe and Dad

Acknowledgments

To all the vendors, providers, users, and friends who have given their time and shared their knowledge, I am very grateful.

Special thanks to my friend Sylvia Charp, and with fond remembrance of Sol, for their encouragement, and our long-running intellectual challenge.

Thanks to Jono Hardjowirogo, my editor at M&T Books, whose belief in this project helped me to overcome health, fire, and flood disasters that occurred during its course.

And thanks to Sheryl Hines, for the many hours of creative input in designing and producing more than 100 illustrations.

CONTENTS

Contents

Contents

Contents

CONTENTS OF FIGURES

INTRODUCTION

The International Telecommunications Union (ITU), formerly the Consultative Committee for International Telephony and Telegraphy (CCITT), had recognized the need for a network plan that would satisfy a wide range of service requirements within a universal broadband standard. This was a new era; we were in the enlightened 1980s, trying to make sense of the vast and sweeping changes of the Information Age. It was a chaotic time. People of vision were predicting exciting new concepts which were directly dependent upon the flow and the application of information in devices that would touch every aspect of our lives. There were expectations of cultural and economic transformations and heightened anticipation of global events that would effect international communications. Looking back, it was a logical time to plan for the future.

Historically, a different specialized network type was developed to satisfy the unique requirements of each information service. Plain Old Telephone Service (POTS), Packet Switched Data Network (PSDN), and Community Antenna Television (CATV) are examples of some diverse networks, specifically designed for the information each carried. The reason for the diversity was fairly simple from a technology standpoint, also considering that separate industries, in developing these networks, were aiming at different objectives. But this strategy meant that spare capacity on one network could not readily be adapted to carry other forms of traffic.

POTS, the public telephone network, was designed for voice services. Although POTS could support low-speed data, this was only possible when the subscriber loop was connected to specific terminal equipment. The PSDN, an effective data transmission service, hasn't quite overcome delay issues which are problematic for voice transmission. Neither POTS nor PSDN have the bandwidth necessary for commercial video and CATV was originally implemented as a one-way system, an unacceptable parameter for interactive voice or data.

The concept for a single broadband network was motivated by many factors, including historical developments and the convergence of the computing and communications industries, a fast-forward result of the Information Age. Another important factor was the continuous emergence of new telecommunications services. During the decade or so of the pre- and postdivestiture era of AT&T the array of new equipment and service providers put many telecommunications buyers into "option shock". And there appeared to be no end of proposals for a wide variety of future services, many without clearly defined transport requirements. Some concepts may require only a few information bits for control (telemetry), others may need millions of bytes per second (High Definition Television—HDTV) to function.

Market demands for services like distance learning, video on demand, and Wide Area Networking (WAN) presented a range of different transmission needs. It did not seem practical to continue meeting transmission requirements with separate specialized networks, such as telephone, data, and video, and then develop more of the same for emerging services. The development of an integrated broadband network was clearly seen as a necessary process to satisfy today's growing demand for transmission capacity, meet the requirements of new services, and accommodate future unknown services.

With the introduction of Integrated Services Digital Network (ISDN), the public telecommunications network made the first important step toward the establishment of a standardized global network. ISDN provides for the integration of voice and data transmission on a single access loop. However, ISDN is a narrowband service and cannot be easily or economically adapted for broadband services, such as video.

Another important issue affecting broadband planning was the rapid progression of developments and improvements in chip technology. As the chip grew in power and functionality, more of the typical network activities were being placed in premises terminal equipment, i.e., ISDN telephone.

It would be remiss not to comment on the contribution of fiber-optic deployment in the network as a significant element in the execution of a broadband strategy. The attainment of super high transmission speeds and the "clean" performance of the optical systems helped broadband planners to develop the characteristics which became accepted as the broadband standard.

Asynchronous Transfer Mode (ATM) is the optimal solution developed and accepted as the standard for public and private networks to implement and begin their evolution toward the Integrated Broadband Communications Network (IBCN). It is a flexible service available today in either T1 or T3 configurations.

Due to the direction of international standards it is important for everyone to become familiar with the language and principles of ATM and begin to incorporate this information into their own planning process.

This book is an in-depth introduction to what ATM is exactly, as well as where and why this technology originated and emerged as a revolutionary technological breakthrough. ATM is presented both in developmental and deliverable perspectives which are then contrasted with other services that are utilized today. Substantial differences do exist.

This contrast clearly delineates the differences that exist between these current services and ATM, and highlights the real values that can be achieved with ATM as a major part of a user network.

Within that context, actual ATM network users' thoughts, plans, and migration strategies are presented to assist in establishing benchmarks for your own applications. As opposed to including one or two case studies, ATM user insights are positioned throughout the book in direct relation to the manner in which we generally assimilate new information into our own telecommunications environment. Starting with initial user reaction to yet another new telecommunications service, we will follow these users through the decision, planning, and design process, into implementation and results analysis.

CHAPTER ONE

A Brief History of Telecommunications

Telecommunications is a fairly recent term used to describe an industry whose origin is in the primitive modes of telephony and telegraphy. The industry has grown and gone through considerable changes. As new technology became available, systems were modified or dropped; whether advances endured or were short-lived, the industry itself has flourished. It is useful to look back and develop an understanding of some high points that have brought us to where we are today, the reasons for some successes, and why some concepts failed.

Networks and Transfer Modes

TELEGRAPHY

The first transfer mode was actually a kind of manual store and forward system. Telegrams, or messages, were given to an operator who sent them, in their turn, down the line to the next station. The coding was essentially digital, a series of long and short pulses, "keyed" by the operator. The first public message was sent from the

Supreme Court House in Washington, DC to Baltimore, MD in 1844. In Figure 1.1 a sender is keying the internationally recognized signal, SOS.

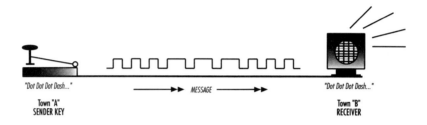

Figure 1.1 Telegraphy's "digital" message.

At each relay station, local messages were delivered to the recipient and others were sent to the next station. The network controlled all functions, including message content. A garbled message initiated a request for retransmission (error correction). As the network grew, centralized stations acted as hubs, relaying messages in many different directions.

Telegraphy was very successful, but its popularity faded with the introduction of that new contraption—the telephone. From the onset, Plain Old Telephone Service (POTS) provided direct conversational contact between the parties, eliminating operator transmission errors, and it was clearly an improvement over the delay in waiting for a reply. Ironically, the telephone enhanced telegraph usage by permitting users to access the telegraph operator from their home or place of business.

Telephony

Telephony introduced a marvelously successful medium and mode of communicating. People were amazed at the concept of direct two-way voice communications with another person in a distant location. Conversation was made possible by connecting subscriber circuits together at one or more switching centers. The circuit of one user, once switched to the circuit of another, is left in place for the duration of the connection (Figure 1.2). Manual switching gave way, first to mechanical switching, then to electromechanical, and finally to electronic switching systems, but the basic Circuit-Switched Transfer Mode (CSTM) has survived. It is undoubtedly the most successful transfer mode introduced, and it still provides the basis for Plain Old Telephone Service POTS. The network was originally responsible for nearly every function, except the conversation.

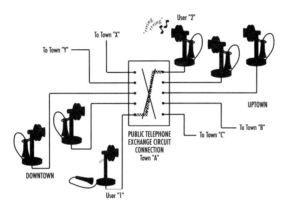

Figure 1.2 Basic concept of telephony.

The conversion to mechanical switches and dial telephones was the beginning of moving some network functions into the hands of the users. The telephone and loop provided an immediate advantage over the telegraph because it gave the user direct network access. Dialing meant that users had rudimentary control over routing and at least shared the responsibility for routing errors, i.e., misdialing.

Public Telephone Network

Voice communication is still the dominant application for Circuit-Switched Transfer Mode (CSTM). The rapid growth in its popularity pushed the widespread implementation of the telephone network. Major communities were the first to have transmission lines linking them to metropolitan centers such as Pittsburgh and Philadelphia. Later implementations connected smaller towns to these communities. Figure 1.3 shows a possible configuration in the early 1900's. The network was soon reaching into the remote regions of this country and nearly every nation on the planet.

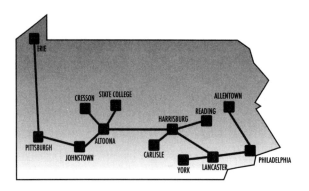

Figure 1.3 A typical early telephone network.

Data Communications

The telephone network was everywhere (not yet ubiquitous), and a new application was emerging with the development of the computer. George Stibitz, an engineer at Bell Laboratories set up what is believed to be the first remote "computer" operation. In 1940, Stibitz used a Teletypewriter to send data from Dartmouth College in Hanover, New Hampshire, to a Bell Laboratories "computer" in New York. This event triggered a new era; it was the beginning of data communications.

The telephone network was a special-purpose network, designed and implemented to optimize analog voice traffic. Use of this network for data traffic was dependent on the development of a terminal device that could modify the digital pulses of data by placing these discrete ones and zeros onto an inherently nondiscrete transmission service. The device became known as a *modem*, a name derived from its MOdulation and DEModulation of digital information bits on an analog carrier frequency. Early versions of the modem were large, bulky, and required a telephone to dial the access numbers (see Figure 1.4), in contrast to modern internal modems with integrated dialing. Fifty-five years later, a very large percentage of terminal connections to computers are still using modems and the telephone network for access. This is despite the differences between voice and data traffic, which led, in part, to the development of the next transfer mode, which was Packet-Switched Transfer Mode (PSTM).

8

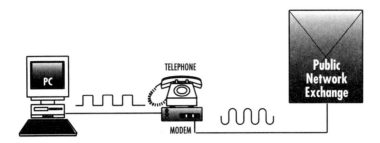

Figure 1.4 A typical external modem for a remote data terminal.

In the Circuit-Switched Transfer Mode (CSTM), the entire end-to-end connection is dedicated to the user. Voice traffic, by the very nature of conversation, occupies about half of the transmission capacity. The balance is idle time, which is a normal part of conversation. In certain long-distance connections, such as via undersea cables between continents, the idle time on a circuit means a larger investment in more circuits. For national long distance services, adding another cable with more circuits was an acceptable investment, but an underseas cable would require a much greater commitment in time, manpower, and cost. Utilization of the idle time would allow the same cable to carry many more conversations. Time Assignment by Speech Interpolation (TASI) was developed to assign idle time to another caller who needed to transmit data. This methodology increases the usage of undersea cables and later is also used in satellite circuits.

Data traffic is referred to as *bursty*—i.e., send, wait, receive— and thus generally has more idle time than voice traffic. However, ready access to the telephone network was a significant economic advantage to most users. The premium paid for idle time was tolerated until a new technology became available that could be used in a network design optimized for the transmission of data traffic.

Packet Switching

Two alternatives were introduced by the Consultative Committee for International Telephony and Telegraphy (CCITT)—packet switching based on the CCITT X.25 protocol and circuit switching based on the

CCITT X.21 protocol—but Packet-Switched Transfer Mode (PSTM) received the greatest support from member nations of the CCITT and thus was more widely deployed.

In Packet-Switched Transfer Mode (PSTM), the resources of the network, or data connections, are not dedicated to the originator/ user. Instead, a communications channel is assigned only for the burst of data traffic. The data message is placed into a packet, complete with addressing and routing information, and is delivered to the network (Figure 1.5). Many packets from many users are slotted on a given channel and sent across the network to the next packet switch. At the switch, locally addressed packets are delivered to the addresses indicated and the rest of the packets are slotted on channels toward their ultimate destinations. Packet switching uses the idle time common to circuit switching, thereby optimizing the network's capacity and increasing overall channel use.

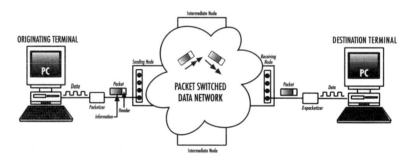

Figure 1.5 Packet-switching basic concept.

Integrated Services Digital Network

With the introduction of Integrated Services Digital Network (ISDN), the public telecommunications network user was introduced to the Synchronous Transfer Mode (STM). STM describes the switching and multiplexing principles that were being used in the telephone networks on the links between switches. The underlying transfer mode in STM, which is used for Narrowband Integrated Services Digital Network (NISDN) is circuit-switched. The user's *circuit* is a time slot in a Time Division Multiplexed (TDM) transmission. Time slots are assigned to users on demand and remain in place for the duration of the call.

Each slot is set up for 64,000 bits, which establishes and limits the user transmission speed to 64 kilobits per second. ISDN extends this time slot to the user on either a 2B+D loop or 23B+D circuit. The *B* refers to a Bearer channel consisting of one time slot, and the *D* channel, another time slot, is reserved for network signaling (9600 bits are available for packet data, if offered by the service provider). Therefore, one ISDN loop consists of three time slots (2B+D) and provides for integration of voice and data transmission on a single access loop. In Figure 1.6, both voice and data are active, while the network signals the user's equipment to generate ringing, indicating a call for the user is in the network.

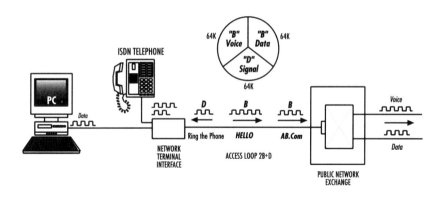

Figure 1.6 A typical ISDN loop in an integrated voice and data application.

In order to allow integrated voice and data on the same loop, the voice signal is converted from its native analog form to a digitized data stream. This digitizing technique is known as Pulse Code Modulation (PCM). The analog signal is sampled 8,000 times per second, with each sample defined by eight bits of data, for a total of 64,000 bits per second. The Bearer channels can be assigned to two voice users or to an integrated voice and data application. Time Compression Multiplexing (TCM), also referred to as the "ping pong" effect, creates the impression of, and for practical purposes is, simultaneous usage.

For higher-speed transmission requirements, certain terminal equipment does provide *bonding* of the Bearer channels, which permits an application to effectively transfer 128,000 bits per second. This capability is effective in many applications including imaging, and providing a reasonable response time.

Private Networks

Until now, the focus has been on the public domain and the events affecting the public network. There are also private networks of different sizes and compositions. The network types are, for the most part, identical to the public networks in terms of transfer modes and functionality. Some private networks are derived from segments of the public network.

Private networks are a matter of choice: economics, privacy, or other owner considerations. Generally, the nature of a private network restricts its relationship to a review of telecommunications. However, all users are affected by network evolution issues, and in the recent past some previously private networks have been opened to public access, i.e., government-sponsored networks.

A very high degree of compatibility between public and private networks is not only sensible, it is desirable. It should be no surprise that in most cases, technological innovations were applied first in the private sector, then by the public sector. Additionally, many teleservice applications promote selective access from public network-based users, i.e., product orders and telecommuting, and they use public network features and information such as Automatic Number Identification (ANI) in their networks. In subsequent chapters, you will see how the private network is involved in the evolution of new international standards.

Transmission Facilities

T1 or DS1

The transmission facilities of public and private networks are comprised of user links and backbone links. A network *user link* is typically connected to a port on a switch or multiplexer, where it is combined with other links to form a network backbone. The *backbone link* interconnects the switch or multiplexer to the next switch or multiplexer in the network. Typical user links are 64 kilobits for multiple low speed or single user medium-speed access, to T1 links for high speed access at 1.544 Megabits, and T3 links for very high speed access at 45 Megabits. Modern digital networks combine these access links in a Digital System Hierarchy (Figure 1.7). While T1 and T3 are designations for a particular carrier type, DS1 and DS3m designate the multiplexing and transmission capability of a system. With this diagram, it can be determined that for very high volume networks a DS3 backbone link, for example, can carry 28 T1 user links.

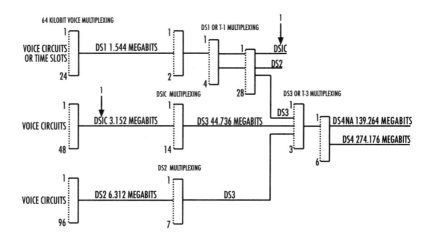

Figure 1.7 Digital system hierarchy.

COMMUNICATIONS SATELLITE

Not long ago, a *satellite* was a moon orbiting a planet. Thanks to Space Age technology, our moon is now one of hundreds of orbiting bodies, most of which are looking toward Earth performing a variety of telecommunications functions (Figure 1.8). The communications satellite is a valuable tool in opening and maintaining global contact.

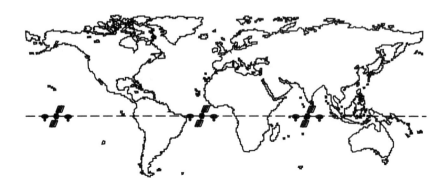

Figure 1.8 Communications satellites in equatorial Earth synchronous orbit.

Because of this important role, the satellite will continue to be a part of both public and private networks. Currently, the satellite is a conduit, carrying terrestrially generated traffic via packet- or circuit-switched transfer modes or both to its intended destination. Future plans may provide for greater functionality on board the satellite itself, such as cell switching for mobile telephones or intersatellite switching. These types of changes will be reflected in both replacement of existing units and the placement of new versions at different altitudes and orbits.

FIBER OPTICS

The contribution of fiber-optic technology in public and private networks can hardly be overstated. The introduction of this medium has dramatically impacted nearly every facet of communications. From the weight and space congestion reduction features up through the almost infinite transmission speeds provided, this technology has more than paid for its developmental investment. Several of the performance characteristics that will be examined later, are attributable to the clean operating behavior of the optical transport architecture. Figure 1.9 shows a fiber-optic segment.

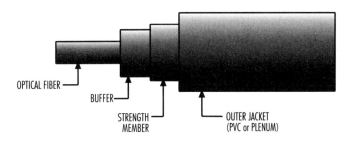

OPTICAL FIBER

BUFFER

STRENGTH
MEMBER

OUTER JACKET
(PVC or PLENUM)

Figure 1.9 Fiber-optic cable composition.

User Networking

LAN, MAN, AND WAN

While most of the changes over the last 100 years have been in the network, the users' premises were not left untouched. The development of the Local Area Network (LAN) substantially improved and enhanced options for flexibility and performance. This development moved in parallel with several equipment and software breakthroughs, which have been standardized by the Institute of Electrical and Electronics Engineers (IEEE) Standard 802.

Early implementations left LAN users "LAN-locked." LAN devices were dedicated to the LAN itself and could not be readily adapted to access other networks. Both modest and substantial changes provided interfaces, gateways, bridges, and routers that freed LAN users and gave way to Metropolitan Area Networks (MAN) and Wide Area Networks (WAN). Figure 1.10 illustrates the relative difference in scope between LAN, MAN, and WAN implementations.

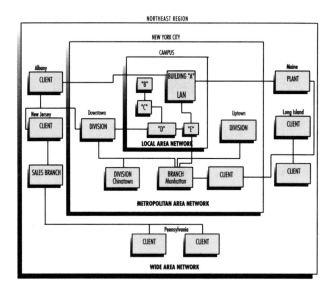

Figure 1.10 Geographic networking hierarchy.

LAN speeds easily outpace those available in the public network link. In many situations, economic or functional considerations are factors that determine MAN and WAN link speeds. Whatever the reason(s), the network interface is an important connection that would benefit from the implementation of a simplified broadband link.

PREMISES WIRING

At the time of AT&T's first divestiture, premises wire and cable installed by the Bell System companies was abandoned in place and became the customer's communications infrastructure; there was virtually no other sensible alternative. The characteristics of this cabling was well suited to voice and data services provided by the Bell System and it was reusable for similar purposes under direct control of the user. For specific applications, such as a Local Area Network (LAN), users installed specific cable types to support these requirements. For example, early LAN implementations were supported on coaxial cable.

The abandoned cable and the customer-installed cable combined to create a veritable "wiring jungle" in terms of appearance, maintenance, and administration. Many communications systems providers introduced structured wiring systems as a way to bypass this jungle. These structured systems featured twisted-pair wiring designed and manufactured to rigid standards is suitable for both voice and high-speed data applications, easier to install, maintain, and administer.

Twisted-pair cable (Figure 1.11) has been joined in offices and buildings and on campuses with high-quality fiber-optic cabling, which gives the sophisticated infrastructure overall multimegabit speeds and near-flawless operation (cockpit errors notwithstanding). The eventual goal is to push this capability past the curb and into the MAN/WAN links.

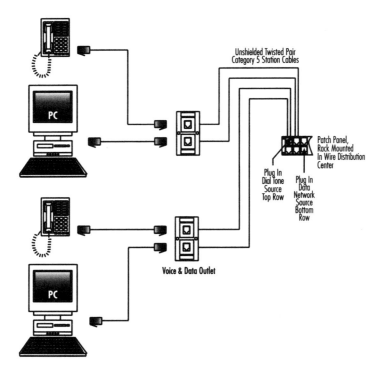

Figure 1.11 Premises wiring, integrated voice, and data.

Regulation and the Market

Technological advances were not the only activities that brought about changes in telecommunications. The most significant change took place in the regulatory and judicial arena. The natural monopoly status of the Bell System had been challenged on several fronts over the past century. The causes that motivated regulators and the judiciary to break up the monopoly is a subject for another day. However, the action of the consent decree, in breaking the Bell System apart, was perhaps the most profound and far-reaching change since the invention of the telephone. Without the decree, the Information Age might have been delayed as a result of the morass, the amalgam formed by the conflicting interests of corporate and regulatory entities, which in past years had slowed the introduction of innovations.

What did result with the decree is that a telecommunications industry is in place today—a vibrant mixture of people, ideas, developments, and services—that caters to both business and residential demands. This renaissance has included the convergence of computing and communications, which generates and fuels itself on technological improvements. The regulatory barriers to innovation no longer prevent technological progress from pushing against convention and toward systems and services that in the past were either impossible to achieve or not cost-effective.

In September 1995, the new AT&T, still a formidable company, decided to "break up" again into three separate multibillion-dollar companies. Perhaps a monolithic structure is not suited to or is unable to move fast enough to answer the challenges generated by today's marketplace. It is hoped that each of the smaller and more targeted companies will be positioned to respond more quickly.

The consumers and users cannot be overlooked in this renaissance. Very quickly, through education and usage, both groups realized the advantages of, and personal benefits to be derived from, the application of telecommunications products and services. Their consumption of the explosion of technological toys and tools offered, together with their expectations for "more, better, faster, and easier," pulls the industry toward greater innovation.

18

Summary

In this chapter, we have briefly touched upon the history and a few of the reasons behind the transformation from what was a collection of unrelated interests to a telecommunications industry. Because it is an industry, with common, or at least compatible objectives, it is shaped by market forces and technological progress. In the next several chapters, we will look at how several of the technologies outlined here, plus the effects of innovation and market demand play a role in shaping policy and strategies in international standards development.

CHAPTER TWO

Developing Asynchronous Transfer Mode

At the time of the Bell System's restructuring, there was a period which can easily be portrayed as chaotic. There seemed to be dearth of activity, directed at an ever-expanding set of problems, on the part of individuals and corporations, resulting in an expanding list of competing products and services, offered by a host of vendors, providers, manufacturers, and systems integrators. Business and residential consumers of these products and services were, in many ways, overwhelmed with developments and choices. But out of this chaos came the winds of change for the telecommunications industry. This period laid the foundation for the technological renaissance which swept the globe and fired imaginations for the Information Age.

The possibilities seemed endless, optimism ran high, and user expectations were unlimited. Technological breakthroughs and mass production in many areas made it possible to economically incorporate computing and telecommunications concepts in a diversity of industries, such as agriculture, protection services, and education. These concepts were for new applications, such as remote weather sensing in agriculture, and new approaches to long-standing requirements, such as dormitory services in educational institutions.

Technology was providing industry with the tools to develop more and better products. With each success, the consumer began to expect more, pushing the industry toward additional developments. With the availability of these new products and the increasing demand for a better device or service, network planners, regardless of the size of the network, were required to look at the transport requirements imposed by, or to be imposed by the introduction of that product or service on their network. But when the introduction of new products and services meant an unacceptable network condition, e.g. , response degradation, the situation clearly needed a solution.

The issues confronting the International Telecommunications Union during this time were similar, yet global in scope and diversity. The need for a single long-term solution to deal with transport requirements imposed by market forces was evident. In order to develop a meaningful solution, the process would have to take into account the present state of telecommunications, address a means of migration to the chosen solution, and present a set of principles that would have sufficient flexibility to adapt to all known and potential unknown requirements. This chapter will look at the criteria used in the creation of the final accepted solution, Asynchronous Transfer Mode (ATM) (Figure 2.1).

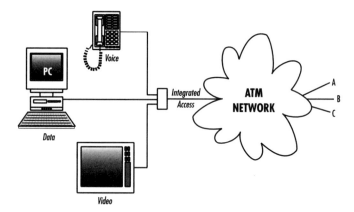

Figure 2.1 The ATM solution.

Network Specialization

In the previous chapter, we looked at the public and private networks which have been characterized as special-purpose networks, optimized for a particular type of traffic. Because of this specialization, modification of a network to accommodate another traffic type is costly, and, as indicated, when modifications *have* been made, they were not always successful. Another point of concern is that each network type is an overlay of an existing architecture (Figure 2.2). As such, there are multiple switching systems, multiplexers, and dedicated interswitch transmission links. To an important degree, specialization requirements also extend to the management, administration, maintenance, and network personnel.

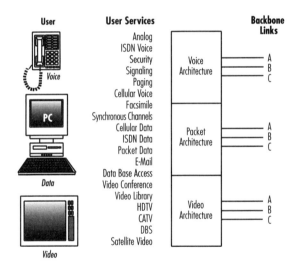

Figure 2.2 The overlay architecture.

The presence of multiple network types, overlaid on the national and international "backbone" also raises the issues of the availability of each network type, the designed capacity of each type, and the consumption of those resources.

The Public Switched Telephone Network (PSTN), for example, is designed for voice traffic with the capacity to handle peak demand, and yet its consumption, or usage, is somewhat sporadic. Though the network is available 24 hours a day, usage is unevenly distributed. For example, the business user's traffic is categorized into hours of usage, the busy hour, or peak demand, representing approximately 20% of the day's calling volume. Typically that day is eight to five o'clock, Monday through Friday. The household traffic pattern is primarily in the evening hours and peak usage occurs on holidays. Therefore, for a large percentage of the year, a vast amount of resources are on reserve for peak calling and not generally available for other services.

Similar examples can be given for other specialized networks, such as cable television systems. A look at programming and scheduling is one way to conclude that "prime time" viewing (usage), during the evening (approximately four hours), is the demand peak in a 24-hour period.

This is not meant to detract from resource-sharing methodologies, which modify the network design, implemented by both users and providers, to allow different levels of sharing. The key word, though, is modification (Figure 2.3). While some level of modification is possible, *and* practical, unlimited modification, though possible, would become unnecessarily complicated and therefore not practical. So, in the end, we have committed resources which cannot be shared across the range of information services.

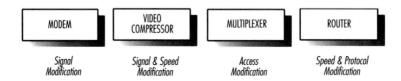

Figure 2.3 Samples of modification devices.

An argument could be made that we have *endless* transmission resources available because of the proliferation of providers and the ever-expanding capacity of fiber optics. While providers, such as carriers and operating companies, have continued to expand their optical systems transmission capacity, a portion of that capacity is for current demand growth, and another large portion of the new capacity will replace aging, less reliable transmission links. In either case, growth or replacement of transmission capacity with optical transport links does not change the specialized multiplexing, switching fabric, or characteristics employed in the current networks. Therefore, we have expanded capacity, but the networks remain specialized.

There is also a trend toward consolidation of the number of providers, as evidenced by the acquisitions, mergers, and partnering now occurring. This simply redistributes the available resources among all surviving providers, who will have accumulated more capacity. But they are still bound to the same specialized switching and multiplexing systems.

Future demand for a network's transport capacity may be easily met, and even surpassed, by the introduction of just a few new services, such as new video services. Video offerings being test marketed by several Bell Operating Companies (BOC) exceed the limits of the POTS network. The subscriber loop itself must be augmented with broadband connectivity in order to have the transport capacity required for such a service. The manner in which the Bell Operating Company designs this service will determine how desired programs are delivered, on demand, for any subscriber, 24 hours a day.

Public Switched Telephone Network

The public switched telephone network, an analog voice network, cannot support all video services. The somewhat limited implementations of Narrowband Integrated Services Digital Network (NISDN) would, in time, upgrade the network to an all digital capability, but, as indicated before, the so-called Synchronous Transfer Mode (STM) is based on a 64K (64,000 bit) time slot. A set of translation tables are used to assign and allocate the slots to various users or functions (Figure 2.4). Although video applications, using compression techniques, are possible with NISDN, it is not a final answer. A standard video signal without compression would need hundreds of consecutive time slots, requiring a large and complex translation table.

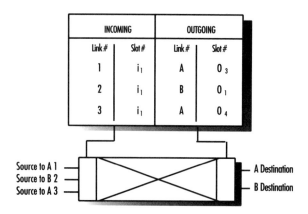

Figure 2.4 Translation table concept.

Consider that the 64K time slot can never effectively utilize other voice coding schemes, such as 32,000 bits in Adaptive Differential Pulse Dode Modulation (ADPCM) or other techniques using lower bit counts. Conversely, a 50 Megabit per second (50Mbps) video service would require an extensive translation table, both complicated and expensive in terms of switching and multiplexing resources.

What could not be clearly defined a decade ago, i.e., BOC video, and what now appears to be on the horizon, i.e., High Definition Television (HDTV) are past and present examples of services with undefined transmission requirements at the outset. If a public or private network is built on a broadband basis suitable for today's video needs, will that network have the switching and multiplexing fabric for HDTV services of the future?

Toward a Single Solution

It seems more practical and more logical to develop a solution that will allow all network resources to be available for all traffic. The current situation of today's networks does not approach this capacity. As seen in the examples given, it is clear that the present architecture is inefficient due to its service dependency and the inability to adapt to different traffic types. From this conclusion, it is possible to begin making assumptions regarding a broadband network at a very basic level so as to make allowances for all traffic types and the specific requirements of each.

The planned broadband network will be required to transport a range of speed and traffic types in support of applications for telemetry, telecontrol, voice, data, video telephony, video library, and remote video education. As a result, the transfer mode for this broadband network cannot be designed for any one service, but rather it must accommodate bit rates and holding times that vary from very low to very high in order to support both known and future unknown services.

An important function of a new broadband network would be end-to-end reliability. From the early days of message handling, it has been the network that performed error correction protocols to ensure that correct information had arrived at its destination. Initial implementations of Packet Switched Data Networks (PSDN), for example, had relatively low-quality transmission facilities, necessitating error correction, including retransmission, on a link-by-link basis (Figure 2.5).

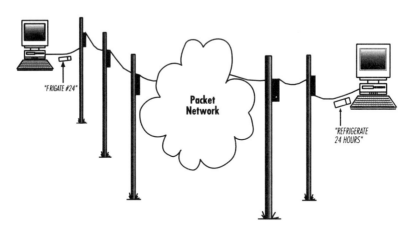

Figure 2.5 The need for error control.

With the implementation of NISDN it was possible to apply system concept logic, taking advantage of improved transmission links and switching systems by limiting error control functions on the link-by-link basis and exerting full error control on an end-to-end basis. A continuation of this system concept, i.e., placing more functions at the network boundary, would remove a substantial degree of complexity from the new broadband network, reducing another important factor—delay.

DELAY

The difference between "time sent" and "time received" is known as *delay*. It is encountered in every stage of the network, including transmission, multiplexing, queuing, routing, and switching. Delay is comprised of two components, transmission delay, which is dependent on the distance traversed on each link, and processing delay, which is dependent on the functions performed by the switching equipment (Figure 2.6).

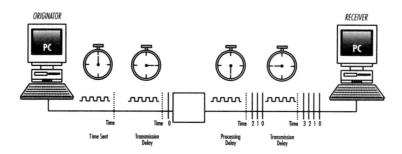

Figure 2.6 The effect of delay.

Real time services, such as voice transmission, suffer tremendously from delay. Echo is one noticeable result experienced by voice users when delay exceeds design parameters. To reduce this effect, echo cancelers were used extensively in analog networks. In the digital network, i.e., NISDN, utilizing circuit switched mode, time relationship is created and maintained in the network in order to guarantee a short delay for all real time services. Time maintenance, of course, adds to the complexity of the network, a complexity not desirable in a multiservice high-speed broadband network. Very high speeds and simplicity in the switching nodes would reduce delay to very small values, and fluctuations of delay, known as "jitter," could also be reduced to very low values.

JITTER DELAY

Jitter is the variation of delay values experienced in different message segments. In the Circuit Switched Transfer Mode (CSTM) discussed above, jitter is near zero in value. But, with Packet Switched Transfer Mode (PSTM) delay and jitter delay values are greater. The complexity of routing, queuing, and switching in the packet switched network limits line speeds and can vary the delay values on a per-packet basis (Figure 2.7). This lack of predictable delay has become an obstacle to the transport of real time services, such as video telephony, on packet networks.

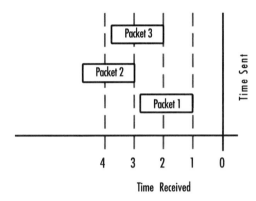

Figure 2.7 Jitter delay results in unpredictable arrival time.

BIT RATES

The goal of a future broadband network is to support all services. As such, a flexible network would have to adapt to bit rates that differ from service to service. The bit rate for both known and future unknown services is contingent on the signal-processing technology used, the coding scheme, and whether any compression technique is applied. When examined in a time relationship, each service will show an average, or a natural and a peak bit rate, which in a general sense can be considered as typical for that service. The differences that exist between these two rates characterize the burstiness of the service.

Bursty Data

Burstiness is a factor in all services, including voice. The burstiness of voice, say at 64,000 bits per second, is clearly seen in the talk and idle times on the circuit. Other services differ considerably from voice. In video, for example, a quality video service at 15 Megabits, frequent bursts of bits may be required to generate movement within a picture.

Viewing a spectrum of services, one can readily conclude that substantial differences exist between the bit rate and the burstiness of the services. An efficient broadband network would look to carry actual information, and not waste resources by bit-stuffing a low bit-rate application on a high bit-rate channel. Resources would also be wasted by using 64-kilobit Pulse Code Modulation (PCM) coding where 32-kilobit Adaptive Differential Pulse Code Modulation (ADPCM) would be satisfactory. And for high bit-rate services, limiting burstiness with a fixed transmission rate would mean discarding some bits at peak rates which, depending on the service, would reduce quality, increase error, or both (Figure 2.8).

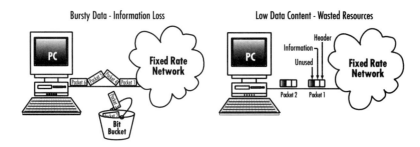

Figure 2.8 Fixed rate network inflexibility.

Network Flexibility

Transport and processing functions, discussed above, are the defining elements of any transfer mode. Transport relates to the transmission facility between network nodes, the user link to the network, and all transmission equipment. To a large extent, the transport functionality is limited by the processing elements. The complexity of the processing functions, primarily switching, therefore, defines the flexibility of a transfer mode. For example, circuit switching provides for a fixed bit rate with little flexibility, while packet switching has the flexibility for a variable bit rate (bursty traffic) but is hindered by low to medium line speed. For an understanding of the development of a high-speed broadband network it may prove interesting to review several switching techniques to see how elements of each may have influenced the development of Asynchronous Transfer Mode (ATM) (see Figure 2.9).

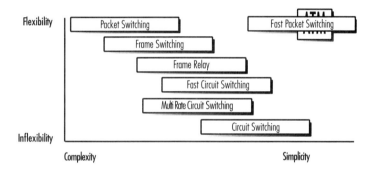

Figure 2.9 Relative ratings of switching technology.

CIRCUIT SWITCHING

Circuit switching is most common to all users. It is the basis for analog and digital telephone service, the latter being Narrowband Integrated Switched Digital Network (NISDN). With NISDN, the circuit is a time slot, set up and controlled by a translation table. Maintenance of the translation table is a switch function, regulating the use of the slot as an element in a Time Division Multiplexed (TDM) frame. For the duration of a connection, a user occupies the same time slot, which occupies the assigned position in the frame (Figure 2.10) on the incoming link to the switch, and a similar assignment on the outgoing link from the switch.

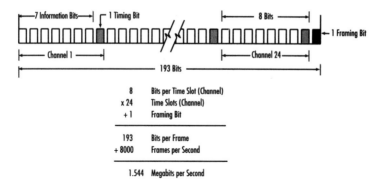

Figure 2.10 The basic transmission frame.

Circuit switching provides a short, predictable delay by maintaining a time relationship (synchronization) within the network. As mentioned earlier, delay is important to real time services, such as voice and video. For voice, the delay in the network must be short, millisecond values, in order to limit the need for echo suppression investments. Since a given connection could entail four switching nodes (originating provider, originating carrier, destination carrier, and destination provider) NISDN switches are designed with delay values measured in microseconds. Longer delays, say in excess of one half-second, may not be problematic for certain one-way services, but delays of this length are detrimental to two-way conversation. A good example of too much delay can be seen in occasional cable talk shows. The host has a remote link, generally satellite, to a guest who, at times, seems to take "forever" to begin responding to the host's questions.

Circuit Switching Errors

Errors in circuit switches are classified as either direct or indirect. Indirect errors are caused by malfunctions in the switch or transmission links (bit errors). Loss of synchronization in the frame is an example of an indirect error, which may cause several consecutive frames to be lost before synchronization is restored. Direct errors are man-made, i.e., protective switching. Protective switching is a network function used to reroute traffic away from switches or links with unacceptably high levels of indirect error. Ironically, information may be lost during this switching operation, causing direct errors.

TIME SLOT CONSIDERATIONS

Although the predictable delay of circuit switching may be a desirable feature, the constant bit rate, established by the fixed time slot, would not be desirable in a broadband network. The ideal broadband network should accommodate a wide range of bit rates. With a circuit switch only one channel size is possible which would require a channel (time slot) to be sized to the highest bit rate to be carried, say 150 megabit. One should readily see, then, that even a 9.6-kilobit transmission would occupy this massive time slot during a connection, creating an unsuitable use of resources, rendering circuit switching unsatisfactory for a universal broadband network.

MULTIRATE CIRCUIT SWITCHING

Multirate Circuit Switching (MRCS) was an attempt to increase the potential bit rates carried. Initial concepts kept the time slot the same size, 64 Kilobits, with the option of, on a per-connection basis, allocating multiple time slots, (up to 30). This option required a substantially more complex switch, since all allocated slots would have to remain synchronized across the network, from source to destination. An enhanced concept placed various fixed slot sizes within an extended frame. While this added bit-sized options, the switching fabric became an overlay of multiple switches, one sized for each of the various bit rates provisioned. In addition, selecting an acceptable bit rate, or set of rates, was problematic. If the rate were set too low, high-speed applications would require a massive channel coordination effort to maintain synchronization. Conversely, a bit rate set too high would waste resources for all low- and medium-speed applications. It would seem, in either case, that resource availability, end to end, would have to be assured before transmission could begin.

As with pure circuit switching, MRCS has a fixed time slot. Regardless of the basic bit rate or various bit rates offered, a fixed rate does not accommodate bursty traffic. This deficiency, combined with resource waste and channel coordination, make MRCS unacceptable within a broadband transport mode.

FAST CIRCUIT SWITCHING

Some time ago, information began to surface about Fast Circuit Switching (FCS). This technique attempted to address the need to handle bursty traffic across a circuit-switched network. Resources were allocated, on demand, via an associated signaling channel. Desired traffic was to be accommodated based on the offered bit rate, or some multiple of that rate. Since resources were not to be allocated in advance, this concept suffered from possible blockages when total traffic offered exceeded switch resources. The need for very rapid setup and knock-down of resources, with notification on a very high-speed signaling link, prevented FCS from getting much beyond the drawing board.

PACKET SWITCHING

More than three decades ago, packet switching was introduced as a data-only networking technology. Variable-length packets enveloped data bits, each packet containing a header field. The network used the header field information for such functions as routing, error control, and flow control. Initially, the transmission links were of marginal quality which necessitated use of complex protocols for link-by-link error and flow control. These protocols are examples of information contained in the header. Packet switching is still very successful for medium- and low-speed data transport, typically for operation at line speeds of 56 kilobits per second or less.

The combination of complexity and line speed presented real time delay problems for packet switching. Delays were relatively long and varied, based on the need for retransmissions. However, packet networks were not intended to carry these types of services, so the delay was not viewed as a major problem. Errors, though, were of great concern which, as stated above, required additional software, adding to the complexity. But as link quality improved it became possible to alter the basic packet switching by eliminating several of the complex functions of X.25, such as logical channel multiplexing, error control, Automatic Resend Request (ARQ), and flow control. Basic packet switching, as described here, could not support all services, therefore it could not be the basis for a universal network.

FRAME SERVICES

The new variations on packet switching are known as Frame Relaying (FR) and Frame Switching (FS). Frame Switching retains all of the X.25 functionality except logical channel multiplexing, and still performs these functions on a link-by-link basis. Network performance can be improved. The extent of improvement with Frame Switching is limited since most of the complexity remains.

Frame Relay services are widely available today for data-only transport. There is a significant performance improvement over packet switching due to the elimination of logical channel multiplexing, error, and flow control. Error detection Cyclic Redundancy Check (CRC), is retained in the network, which allows the network to dump erroneous frames rather than continue to transport them to a destination. Frame relaying also deviates from traditional packet switching by placing retransmission functionality at the boundary of the network, performing this step on an end-to-end basis as needed. This is another example of the systems concept discussed previously, where a function is performed once at the boundary, rather than being repeated multiple times across the network. Although frame services are an improvement over packet switching, these services are intended as data-only methodologies and are not useful as the basis for a universal broadband network.

FAST PACKET SWITCHING

Fast Packet Switching (FPS) is actually a concept with several different alternatives, each based on the principle of minimal functionality in the network. Due to the simplicity of the switching equipment, projected speeds for this concept are much greater than basic packet services. The anticipated line speeds and minimal delay mean that FPS could carry real-time services, and because of the significant reduction in network processing, bursty data and many other applications would be able to make use of this technology. By reviewing several characteristics of this concept the reasons for higher speed and flexibility may become clear.

Resource Allocation

An originating terminal, in the FPS concept, requests allocation of resources from the network, which then logically determines if a reservation can be made: if not, the connection is denied. Packet switching is sufficiently flexible for bursty data and the set-up step virtually assures that all link, switch, and queue facilities are available for the intended transmission, guaranteeing minimum packet loss and maximum transmission quality. At the completion of the transmission session, all facilities are rapidly released for the next originator. The operation described here is similar to circuit switching and is known as *connection oriented mode.*

Flow Control

Flow control and error control are eliminated on a link-by-link basis, due in part to the high quality of the links, but mostly to proper resource provisioning. First, resources are reserved on demand, and secondly, queuing at the switching locations is properly dimensioned. Together, dimensioning and allocation parameters limit potential packet loss to a probability of up to one in a trillion (10^{-12}), thereby eliminating flow control in the network.

Error Control

Errors are less complex in Fast Packet Switching (FPS), even though there are more causes and different types of errors. Single-bit and burst errors can be due to noise, loss of synchronization, or protection switching. The quality of the links and reduced processing functions significantly diminish the incidence of these errors—however, when they do occur, the network takes no corrective action; instead FPS relies on boundary-based protocols.

Fast Packet Switching Header

The primary function of the header is routing. At set-up time a header identifier is selected for defining the virtual channel to permit proper routing of the packets. The remaining functions of the header are limited to maintenance, header error detection, and an error correction technique intended to reduce routing errors. A direct result of simplicity in the header processing is that processing speeds can be increased to the Gigabit level resulting in very low queuing and processing delays.

SWITCHING DELAYS

Within the switching fabric, the queuing delay is a function of packet size. The queue buffers can be kept small by using a small packet and a short header, e.g., limited header functionality and a small information field. In addition to the economy of smaller buffers, the network gains in reduced queuing delays and delay jitter values satisfactory to real time services.

FAST PACKET SWITCHING CONCLUSIONS

From the above discussion, the switching methodology which seems to have the desired characteristics for a broadband network is FPS. In fact the alternative name given to FPS by the International Telecommunications Union (ITU) is Asynchronous Transfer Mode (ATM) (Figure 2.11), which, as a concept, has been refined and developed by the member nations and selected as the transfer mode for the Integrated Broadband Communications Network (IBCN). However, several issues had to be resolved before that decision could be made.

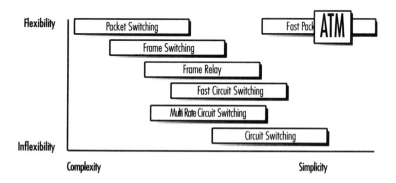

Figure 2.11 Positioning Asynchronous Transfer Mode.

Network Transparency

These issues dealt with characteristics which affected time and semantic transparency. Time transparency deals with delivery of originating information from its source to its destination in a time satisfactory to the application. Semantic transparency is a measure of the accuracy of the information sent compared to that which was received. These have been discussed previously in terms of delay and error. Here delay and error are discussed in relation to the specific performance expected from an ATM network with respect to these two basic factors.

TIME TRANSPARENCY

On an end-to-end network, delay is accumulated from many sources. In a pure ATM network, those sources are explained below:

Packetization Delay (PD) occurs when originating traffic is enveloped in the information field of the ATM packet which has a header coded for the packet's transport. Using a short packet aids in keeping this value low (Figure 2.12).

Transmission Delay (TD) is encountered on each link the packet must traverse. This delay is inherent on any link, regardless of the transfer mode, and is typically a low single-digit microsecond value (Figure 2.12).

Switching Delay (SD) is composed of two elements, a Fixed Delay (FD) to account for the packet passing through the switch architecture, and Queuing Delay (QD) to account for the time expended by the packet as it waits in the buffers for processing. Fixed Delay is switch design dependent, while Queuing Delay (QD) is load dependent. Since real time services are affected most by delay parameters, the total Switch Delay is kept low to meet these requirements, as discussed earlier in this chapter (Figure 2.12).

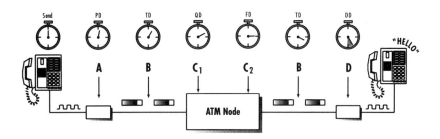

Figure 2.12 Asynchronous Transfer Mode delay factors.

Depacketization Delay (DD) is the time required to restore the ATM packet to the original bit stream form, e.g., voice from the ATM packet to an Integrated Services Digital Network (ISDN) synchronous bit stream. Real-time services may have some delay introduced at the receiving terminal in order to mask the jitter delay which may have been introduced in the ATM network. The restored bit stream can then be synchronized as it was before packetization.

Until a single universal network exists, it is important to note that some ATM implementations will have interconnectivity with other network types. In these situations, additional delay will be encountered at each ATM network boundary in the form of packetization and depacketization delays. Overall transport delay will be the total of all delay elements encountered in the interconnected networks.

Parameters that affect delay are critical in determining the time transparency of an ATM network in relation to real time applications, such as voice or video. The issues discussed below have a direct impact on the delay values presented here and could result in situations that require echo cancelers or, with sufficiently high delay values, impair the application's quality.

Packetization Delay

The bit speed generation of the originating device, coupled with the packet size (to be discussed later), can introduce delay values from low milliseconds for 64 Kilobit to microseconds for Megabit speeds.

Fixed Delay

A switch designed for ATM speeds of 150 Megabits or greater will have values dependent on packet size. For the size considered in these parameters, the delay will be in low microsecond values per switch (per exchange, or node).

Queuing Delay

The switch architecture, the size of the queues, and traffic load are factors which will affect the value of this delay. Considering the speed of the switch, dimensioning of queues, a small packet size, and maintaining load limits below 100% it is possible to keep this delay below millisecond values.

Depacketization Delay

Depacketization delay is the time required to restore the bit stream to its pre-ATM state. Also, there is the introduction of additional delay for real time services, to smooth the delay jitter. Since jitter is a function of the queuing variations, it is not uncommon to see the two values combined and charted together. Expectations are for very low millisecond to microsecond values.

It seems likely from this discussion that a high-speed broadband network, based on ATM principles, will have an end-to-end delay value in the low millisecond range, suitable for real-time services and limited implementation costs for echo cancelers.

SEMANTIC TRANSPARENCY

The semantic transparency of an ATM network is an important issue if we are to consider a network without error and flow control. The network then must possess the characteristics necessary to transport information with a very low probability of error or loss. Error and flow control problems from transmission, switching, multiplexing, and load in an ATM network, differ from traditional packet switching and require careful consideration.

PACKET LOSS

Packets lost due to queue overflow affect all services. For ATM, the expected low value for Packet Loss Ratio (PLR) of 10^{-12} surpasses the acceptable ratios for known services, and allows some margin for future services with more stringent requirements. First consider that the ATM network operates in a connection-oriented mode, meaning that sufficient network resources and current load must be in place before granting a connection. Second, if proper dimensioning of the queues can guarantee an easily achievable minimum ratio of 10^{-8} (Figure 2.13), i.e., the acceptable Packet Loss Ratio for video, the PLR requirements for other services, which are not as severe, will be met.

10^{-8} 10^{-3}

Figure 2.13 A range of acceptable packet loss ratios.

ATM Error Control

The ATM network has no error control on a link-by-link basis for transmission bit errors in the information field. Correction and recovery for these errors is a terminal function, on an end-to-end basis, transparent to the network. But error correction and detection in the header is essential to preventing packet loss and misrouting. The ATM header is small and so keeps processing time low. Bit space is not available for error methodologies such as those found in traditional packet switching (which require a larger header and more processing time). In short, the concept is to detect single bit errors in the header only, correct that error, then move on. In the case of burst errors, where the header is small, and particularly with a short packet, multiple header errors and information errors will occur, perhaps in several consecutive packets. Since only single errors are corrected, the packet or packets with the corrupted header(s) would be discarded.

The result for the ATM network is that single bit errors in the header will be corrected and multiple errors in the header, due to bursts, will cause the packet to be discarded. Quality transmission links and switching equipment (Figure 2.14) will minimize single and burst error occurrences limiting total packet loss to very low values.

Packet Switching		ATM
Link-by-Link		End-to-End
Low	Quality of Links & Switching	High
>	Error Control	<
>	Network Complexity	<
Kilobits	Transmission Speed	Gigabits

Figure 2.14 The effects of ATM quality links and switching.

FIXED VERSUS VARIABLE LENGTH

Packet length and the question of whether fixed or variable sized packets should be selected are two additional issues to be resolved. One alternative in the Fast Packet Switching (FPS) concept opts for short fixed-length packets, while another opts for variable lengths. Switching efficiency and processing speed are directly affected by these options, as has been discussed previously.

FIXED-LENGTH PACKETS

The broadband network is intended to carry all types of traffic, i.e., voice, data, and video, and must therefore be optimized for a spectrum of services rather than specialized for one service. Optimal efficiency is found in full packets. Voice and video, with fixed-rate coding, are continuous bit-rate services. To fill the packet with ISDN voice, for example, bit generation is relatively slow so the information field needs to be small to minimize packetization delay. Video bits are generated rapidly, filling small packets quickly. Both services, as described, will come close to optimal efficiency. Video with variable-rate coding will not differ greatly from the fixed rate efficiency level mentioned above, filling small packets quickly, due to the speed of bit generation and high volume of bits generated.

Data, though, is a mixture of services, from keyboard generation to file transfer, with low to high efficiency, respectively. Packet fill would vary from several bytes to a full packet. Looking at the combined traffic from all services and the use of a small fixed packet, it can be concluded that the network could function with a high optimal efficiency.

VARIABLE-LENGTH PACKETS

Variable-length packets would need a larger header to define their length, and also require packet delimiter flags. Adding bits to the header increases processing delay and complexity, both detriments to network speed. Very long packets may have a high efficiency, but some limit needs to be applied due to queue dimensioning, processing overhead, and delay.

While the high efficiency of variable-length packets is attractive, the ATM network carries a mix of traffic types, essentially trimming the efficiency gain derived from the variable-sized packets. The fixed packet became the popular choice, with the understanding that for certain applications some variation might exist.

NAME AND SIZE ISSUES

Remember the argument "If it looks like a duck, quacks like a duck," etc.? Well, it looks like a packet, but it is fixed in length, and, in order to mark the distinction, the fixed-length packet in an ATM network has been renamed. It is known as a *Cell*, an appropriate retronym. This distinction between a packet and cell is perhaps more apparent in the resolution of the cell size issue.

Cell length will have an impact on transmission efficiency, delay, and the overall complexity of network implementation. Arguments presented earlier, with regard to each of these issues, point to a short cell length, in particular when consideration is given to transport distance, the number of nodes that could be encountered, header size, buffer dimensioning, processing overhead, and echo cancelers. In the end, cell size was a compromise at 53 bytes, 5 bytes for the header and 48 bytes for the information field.

Conclusion

From the above discussions, it is clear why Asynchronous Transfer Mode (ATM) is the set of principles upon which one universal network will be built, the Integrated Broadband Communications Network (IBDN) (Figure 2.15). Over the last century and a half, change, technology, growth, regulation, and the marketplace have played an important role in the evolution from a diversity of enterprises to a telecommunications industry. However, the transport infrastructure is fragmented with an overlay of specialized architectures offering limited resource sharing across information types. The existing transfer modes underlying these architectures have been shown to lack the flexibility necessary to easily adapt to the unstoppable demand for new services, many of which may have incompatible transmission requirements. ATM is a logical step which provides the means to combine diverse technologies and move the industry into the future with a common international standard.

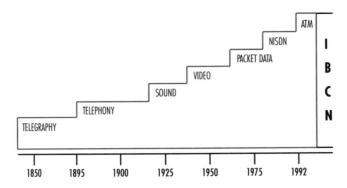

Figure 2.15 Telecommunications industry evolution.

Other advantages of having one universal network are easy to see.

- Everyone will benefit from the economies of scale derived from the likely cost reductions experienced by manufacturers and providers following a single standard.
- A significant gain in efficiency is derived because the ATM network permits all resources to be used by any service, including real time and bursty applications traffic.
- The flexibility crucial to a universal network is demonstrated by ATM's successful adaptation to emerging services without changes in switching systems, multiplexers, or transmission links, and there are no foreseen changes required for the unknown services of the future.

CHAPTER THREE

An ATM Environment

Applying New Technology

While looking at new technology and new services, it is natural to think about how that technology or service could be useful in our own environment, and to consider its potential results there. This chapter will provide an opportunity to accelerate this process by reviewing various telecommunications environments and briefly discussing the issues facing the users. These user applications and network issues will approximate your own with respect to user requirements, network complexities, and the challenges they present. The backgrounds, situations, and issues presented are of interest and should be useful in gauging the possible application of an ATM solution (see Figure 3.1).

Figure 3.1 The ATM network solution.

Over the next several years, Asynchronous Transfer Mode (ATM) will become an integral part of nearly every user environment. Several of the user organizations included here have already migrated to ATM. (Their identities, however, will not be disclosed, since the purpose of this chapter is to look at application needs in a general sense.) The goal is to uncover a set of practical conclusions which are relevant to ATM technology.

User A: Background

A group of 30 traders and salespeople in an investment banking firm were responsible for transactions in the taxable fixed-income market. This involves agreements to repurchase securities from buyers, for a specific price, with the transaction to be executed at a future time. In 1989, the group implemented a single-segment Ethernet with thirty 386SX PCs and server to introduce a 'repo' trading system. As business volume grew, traffic on the network increased beyond expectations. The applications software includes four custom-designed packages for real time trading. The data stored on the server is a combination of 'repo' pricing and analytics, deal capture, trade matching, and position-keeping applications. Intending to improve response time, provide for transaction growth and network performance, the network was upgraded to a dual-segment FDDI, with thirty-five PS/2 clients, running DOS, with a PS/2 server and Novell NetWare v3.11.

USER A: SITUATION

In the first year on the Ethernet LAN, transaction volume was more than double the projected network traffic. In the second and subsequent years transaction volume continued to climb upward (see Figure 3.2). Upgrading the network gave only temporary relief, as volume continued to increase. Response-time degradation was becoming more noticeable on the shared-media FDDI network. Also, projections for trading activity in the coming year were compounded by the introduction of a "daylight overdraft" imposed by the Federal Reserve Bank. The overdraft is a per-minute fee imposed on transactions to encourage rapid transfer of the money involved. With this fee, an added burden is placed on the network in the form of more activity and greater time sensitivity attached to each transaction.

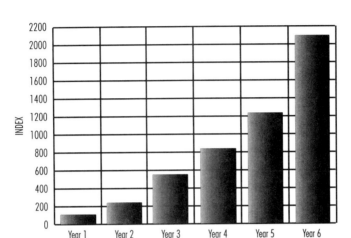

Figure 3.2 Network traffic indices.

USER A: ISSUES

Before the overdraft requirement was introduced, the user was faced with an increasing volume of traffic, bringing with it a noticeable increase in response delay. More important, the issue became one of how to handle the current volume faster, so as to minimize the cost implications of the new fee. However, with expectations for continued business growth, a second issue was to find capacity for that growth while maintaining the necessary time efficiency.

USER A: ANALYSIS

In this LAN environment, using a shared media, all traffic traverses the media to its destination. Delay is dependent on network load, and response times will vary, based on the traffic load. Peak loads would further degrade response time. Additionally, the FDDI network, as designed, has a maximum capacity of 100 Megabits. With an ATM LAN switch, the user has a direct connection to a nonblocking architecture. Traffic is processed with a nearly consistent delay expectation, regardless of the load offered by other users. Access speeds are available at 155 Megabits, with migration opportunities to higher rates that will continue to accommodate growth.

User B: Background

Large financial institutions with hundreds of branch offices are commonplace today. This user has, through merger and acquisition, become a full-scale financial services provider, operating in multiple states. For the purpose of this discussion, the focus is on their branch banking, which is undergoing a transformation from an extension of the main bank, to a showcase retail outlet geared toward customer satisfaction. With hundreds of retail locations, the user is heavily dependent on telecommunications services provided by several different Local Exchange Carriers (LEC) and interexchange transport from a major service provider. Branch locations range in size from several hundred square feet of secure space in a retail chain, to several thousands of square feet in malls, office complexes, and stand-alone buildings. Regardless of the outlet's size, the telecommunications functionality and access requirements are nearly identical. A typical branch requires access for voice, multiple data types, and security (see Figure 3.3).

Figure 3.3 Banking access requirements.

User B: Situation

Retail automation is one of the key elements in providing enhanced customer service. Also, standardization of the technologies employed will facilitate the expansion, or redistribution of the retail outlets. Pre-automation access is via a low-speed multiplexing modem on dedicated circuits to the centralized control. An updated retail outlet augments base technologies with enhanced security and surveillance, digital telephony, substantially increased data transport, and several levels of conferencing, including video teleconference (see Figure 3.4). While traditional centralization of services still exists, the customer's service interface, whether a person or a machine, is fully distributed in the retail store.

Figure 3.4 Enhanced banking access requirements.

USER B: ISSUES

Telecommunications services are vital to this operation. It is essential to have adequate access and transport in each location to provide the "front office" customer service and the "back office" customer support capabilities featured in the new retail facility. Upgrading the limited function data terminal system to a client/server network will change access requirements and affect the present multiplexing procedures. Among the access requirements are low-speed security, medium-speed voice, high-speed data, and very high-speed video. With hundreds of retail locations to be upgraded, the optimal choice for access will have to be cost-effective and highly reliable.

USER B: ANALYSIS

Shared access, as discussed in this environment, is one of the design parameters of ATM. Voice, data, video, and security signaling data streams are loaded into their cells independent of each other, and routed individually as directed by the Virtual Path Identifier (VPI) and VIrtual c hannel Identifier (VCI) addressing. In the absence of a Local Exchange Carrier (LEC), or private fiber provider's metropolitan ATM/SONET network which would provide the highest reliability and best recovery options, a third choice may be feasible, depending on traffic volume. A T1 ATM network, interconnected to an Interexchange Carrier's (IXC) ATM backbone, would provide regional connectivity, on a per-LEC or a per-state basis, to the institution's centralized control location(s). Retail outlets could be added, deleted, and moved with limited network reconfiguration. Additionally, the branch's local voice traffic would continue to use the local POTS network, but, on a per-location basis, long distance voice traffic could be sent on the ATM network, to a centralized "least-cost routing" platform.

User C: Background

This health care provider has carefully developed a strong regional presence through merger and partnering in a large, mostly rural, geographic area. During this period, the growth and deployment of telecommunications technologies evolved in an applications-specific, departmentalized manner with emphasis placed on tactical efficiency. With physical expansion, employment growth, and changes in health care services, a more strategic consciousness is directing the implementation of applications and technologies. File servers have been used to support user communities and assist in limiting the extent of traffic that traverses the shared backbone. Internetworking changes and upgrades to individual systems were structured to augment total internetworking for any user. When off-campus space was occupied by hospital personnel, a Metropolitan Area Network (MAN) was implemented, utilizing T1 connectivity (see Figure 3.5). Bandwidth is shared by voice services, extended from the PBX, and data access is provided to campus-based resources.

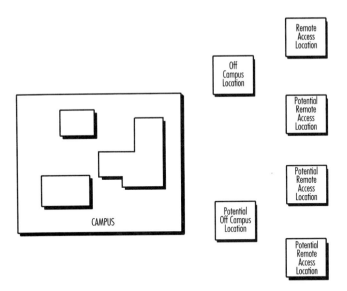

Figure 3.5 Hospital complex.

USER C: SITUATION

The administration and medical staffs are pleased with the operation and functionality afforded by the wide array of applications
now automating workflow and improving productivity. Information
systems (IS) is generally pleased as well. However, as in any IS
organization, knowledge of certain inherent weaknesses is fuel for
strategic planning programs. The IS staff, like most staffs of this
size and complexity, are burdened with day-to-day operations and
problem solving, which leaves little or no time for planning
improvements (see Figure 3.6).

Network servers are bogged down, directing traffic across a
fragile architecture that has too many single points of failure. The
structural deficiencies lead to cross-traffic and device-location irreg-
ularities. Troubleshooting problems, network administration, and
management are more complicated and time consuming than they
need to be. The off-campus MAN is at capacity. Attempts to provide

bandwidth relief, and backup facilities, with microwave links were less than satisfactory.

A new application, for remote access to specific files, was recently implemented on Centrex ISDN. Other applications are near roll-out as well; however, the fundamental problems of the internal network remain.

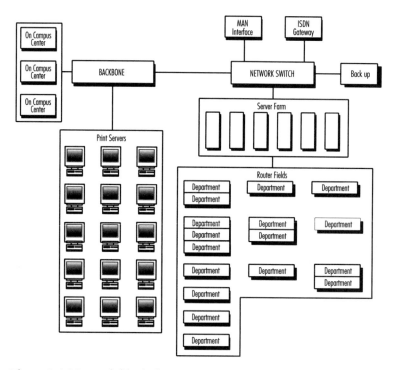

Figure 3.6 Network block diagram.

USER C: ISSUES

In today's climate, it is easy to understand a cost-conscious attitude in health care professionals and Information Systems organizations. With federal, state, insurance, public, and industry watchdogs scrutinizing health care expenditures, administrators and IS professionals utilize technology in a cost-effective manner in accordance with industry standards. At various levels, both internal and external, cost justification can be a critical issue. Since the administration and staff are pleased with the functionality and response they are receiving today, it falls to the IS personnel to use the network weaknesses to demonstrate the need for change based on assumed risks.

USER C: ANALYSIS

The MAN being used for voice and data traffic is at capacity. The voice channels in the T1 are dedicated (about 50% of the capacity). ATM technology would allow more of the total bandwidth to be used at all times when voice traffic volume is low, potentially making about 25% more (approximately 380 Kilobits) of this MAN's capacity available to data users.

In the main complex, ATM LAN switching could take over the routing functions being performed by the servers, and provide a higher-speed backbone network. By adding LAN emulation to the ATM switch, existing departmental network and system investments can be protected. The transparency of the ATM switch would also relieve much of the system interdependencies that exist, and provide an alternative for device location. For new applications, the ATM LAN switch can be upgraded to speeds in excess of 155 Megabits, and provide access for off-campus applications with interface speeds that will match the ATM networking standards, i.e., T1, T3, OC3.

User D: Background

The gap between the research laboratory and commercial application of the federal government's defense technology is being bridged by "Centers for Excellence" such as User D. This non-profit corporation, with multiple centers, is working with a wide range of applications for use in manufacturing, and plans to include distributed parallel computing and virtual reality simulation. Each center utilizes high-powered workstations, interconnected with an Ethernet LAN, to support their computation-intensive applications (see Figure 3.7). Although the centers are focused on different sets of issues, because of the sophistication of the applications and the interdisciplinary relationships between the centers, there is a heavy reliance on the organization's network.

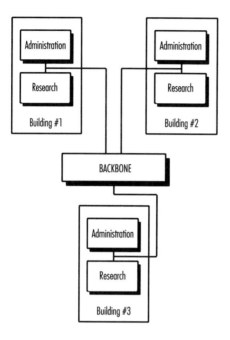

Figure 3.7 Campus network block diagram.

USER D: SITUATION

The transport capacity of the existing LAN is near capacity with the current applications. With plans to develop interactive, distributed, three-dimensional modeling and desktop video conferencing, there is concern for the Ethernet LAN's ability to carry the additional load.

USER D: ISSUES

Interactive modeling and video conferencing, mentioned above, are good examples of applications which will become more commonplace in the work environment by the turn of the century. Because of the high bandwidth, low delay, and deterministic response time requirements, any of the typical LAN architectures would be challenged if these two applications were added to an already busy network.

USER D: ANALYSIS

This campus network environment is now expected to transport a much greater volume of traffic, and provide a low-delay and high-quality performance for the new applications. Users will be demanding rapid response times for both interactive and video conferencing applications. Developing defense technologies to commercial uses may also give rise to future applications which today have unknown transmission requirements. ATM technology provides the high-speed and deterministic response times required by this user. The ATM LAN switch is designed for the campus environment, and its network emulation capabilities are intended to allow the Ethernet to co-exist for administrative applications.

User E: Background

This organization provides reliable state-of-the-art data communications services to the globally dispersed resources of a government research community. The intent of the network is to foster collaboration among the researchers at national laboratories and participating universities. Another important part of the service is to provide for shared access to expensive resources, such as supercomputers and mass data storage facilities. In early 1990, the initial network was introduced using T1 backbone circuits interconnecting 19 U.S. laboratories. User access is through a variety of methods, to routers at the backbone sites. The routers are equipped for several protocols, such as Internet Protocol (IP), DECnet Phase IV, and Open Systems Connection-Less Network Protocol (OS/CLNP). The majority of traffic is IP. Currently there are 24 labs, selected backbone segments have been upgraded to T3 circuits, and interfaces have been established to other national and international networks, increasing global access to researchers and resources (see Figure 3.8).

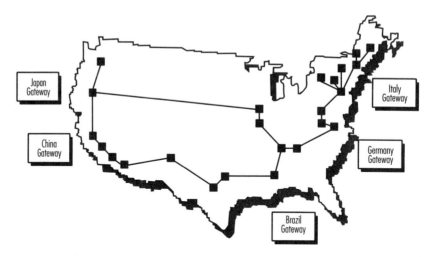

Figure 3.8 User E network diagram.

USER E: SITUATION

The network supports multiple-program, open scientific research, and necessary information dissemination throughout the user population. Since its introduction the traffic has grown steadily, tracking closely with the traffic growth on the Internet. The network is monitored and controlled, every day, all day and night to maintain the quality and accessibility needed to satisfy the global user population. Network statistics are routinely gathered to assist in troubleshooting and long-term planning. Over time, the network will provide new services to users and incorporate new technologies in the network as they become available and economically feasible. Examples added include an X.500-based user directory, on-line information access over several interfaces, and ISDN multiparty video conferencing services.

USER E: ISSUES

In 1992, the federal government's High-Performance Computing and Communications program provided funding to increase the cooperative interaction between government and private industry. The purpose is to enhance competitiveness in networking technology and accelerate the pace of technological innovation. This mandate provides the impetus to structure new services on the network to ensure the success of the program. New services would include distributed computing, interactive modeling, and cooperative applications software development. With each new service, transmission requirements and network flexibility, in the areas of changing traffic loads and the diversity of potential new interfaces, would be potential problems on the existing leased-circuit network.

USER E: ANALYSIS

With the preponderance of traffic being IP, ingress and egress of that traffic is provided for in the ATM Adaptation Layer 5 (AAL 5) protocol, standardizing the interface. T3 links are already in place, which could simplify the transition to ATM on the backbone for this user. The addition of new applications, some of which may have unknown transmission requirements and traffic peak loads, will be more easily facilitated in an ATM network due to improved bandwidth utilization and the independence of the data streams, e.g., voice, data, and video-on-video conferencing setups. Additionally, expanding network access to business and industrial constituents would be accommodated more readily with ATM technology because of the available mix of standard interfaces, e.g., Frame Relay and T1 Emulation. An ATM/SONET backbone would improve network monitoring, survivability, and network restoration in the event of a failure.

User F: Background

Providing engineering services for the design and maintenance of nuclear power systems is the primary focus of this organization. The complexity and critical nature of these systems creates massive computer files, typically tens of megabytes. Computing is done on a supercomputer running batch programs which can run as long as 10 hours. Data files generated as a result of these programs may be as large as hundreds of megabytes.

USER F: SITUATION

Supercomputers are expensive and primarily intended for massive batch-oriented jobs. Costs for operating and maintaining their supercomputer are well into millions of dollars per year. Current productivity, calculated in "compute resource units," an internal mechanism used to measure the effectiveness of workflow, peaks near the maximum. The maximum compute resource units in any given month are 47,000. Cost, batch-optimization, and the current business load appear to be impediments to developing interactive applications, such as visualization software.

USER F: ISSUES

The decision to migrate to a distributed network of powerful workstations is based principally on the concept of saving money. Introducing workstations on a distributed computing network (see Figure 3.9) would require a substantial transport capability to provide for interactivity, and to provide for peak traffic loads. Also, current batch programs would have to be modified to develop the interactive applications and graphical user interfaces.

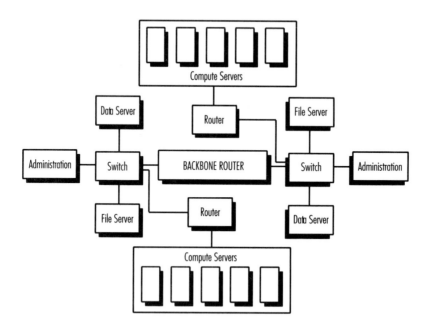

Figure 3.9 Distributed computing block diagram.

USER F: ANALYSIS

To convert this supercomputer operation to a distributed network of "super" workstations, the network must be robust enough to transport the huge computer and data files discussed above. For file transfer, the ATM technology initially provides 155 Megabits and has expected speeds up to 2.4 Gigabits. At this high end, data files generated by the batch programs, e.g., 100 megabytes, would be transmitted in fractional seconds. A high-speed ATM LAN could promote the co-existence of batch files, interactive data, and fluctuating business volume in a distributed network.

User G: Background

This company is a relatively new designer and manufacturer of communications and networking products. The organization was formed to become a part of the leading-edge introduction of new high-performance networking products and services. The company has grown rapidly from a single facility operation into a multi-location, multi-function web of administration, design, manufacturing, and sales locations in domestic and foreign countries. The facility growth has been necessitated by the expanding client list, and the addition of personnel to provide engineering, production, sales, and support functions at the remote offices.

USER G: SITUATION

The rapid expansion is a result of acquisitions, mergers, and strategic alliances that not only increased personnel, but each added another layer of communications complexity with respect to the now distributed functions of the business. The installation of T1 WAN interconnected the major centers to support engineering functions and improve the internal communications, e.g., E-mail, fax, and voice traffic among support offices utilize POTS access for reaching their regional center, which can also provide network access to other centers. Foreign offices hone in on the headquarters location for their internal communications and network access. Negotiations to further growth and expansion are at various stages, from initial inquiries to finalization.

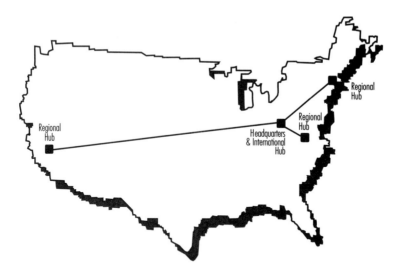

Figure 3.10 Wide Area Network.

USER G: ISSUES

Given the pattern for change, this user is encountering myriad issues, including location. Location speaks to the dilemma faced by many users, that is, the capability of the LEC in that locale, foreign or domestic, to provide networking options that urban and metropolitan users take for granted. Another facet of acquisition and mergers is the disparity that exists between embedded systems. With dynamic executives driving a steep growth curve, the operating directors are hustling to meet the communications needs of today's business, and, at the same time, provide capacity to implement distributed applications necessary for sustaining growth.

USER G: ANALYSIS

Corporate centers and enterprise zones don't always fall within the boundary of progressive LECs, nor within quality access to conventional networking, let alone access to new technology. The IXCs are working to implement LEC and international ATM interfaces which will support the needs of all users, including User G. The IXC can reach inside the LEC to provide dedicated connectivity, but is often dependent on the LEC for installation and maintenance support such as the existing T1 WAN. The obvious solution, ATM networking, is the direction that should be pursued for headquarters and the regional centers. The size and scope of the smaller remote offices, with few people, and little office time (sales and support people on the road), introduces the potential of a migration strategy, such as Frame Relay, where available, internetworked with the ATM sites.

Conclusions

The above users were selected for their commercial and network diversity. While this exercise is based on brief descriptions, it is intended to list known requirements and user issues that facilitate thinking about ATM technology in actual situations. For these users, demand, growth, new applications, future applications with unknown requirements, response time, and multiple access are specific requirements. These requirements point to the design parameters of ATM that are applicable to each of the user environments presented.

ATM is not yet a total solution—equipment and protocol issues are still being resolved. The standards, though, identify the targets of manufacturers and network providers. With each passing day, week, month, or quarter, another of these standards targets is hit by someone. It seems appropriate to begin to consider how ATM will fit into your user environment, and the issues there which this technology will address.

Summary

If there were an opportunity to discuss only one facet of the telecommunications industry that has undergone a significant change, the *user environment* would certainly deserve consideration. Tremendous changes have taken place here, and it is also here that needs and demands have forced these changes. The user in this environment is the information worker, the chief information officer, the systems analyst, and all the people touched by telecommunications products and services for voice, data, and video. The environment is the desktop, the IS department, the home office, the automobile, aboard ship, and any place suited to the use of those same products and services. It is these users, and in these environments, who have learned to apply technology to find solutions for manufacturing, commercial, government, education, and medical problems; who have found enjoyment in the leisure and learning available across the electronic landscape. It is these users who have set aside the almighty "pen" for the more timid, yet creative "mouse," the telephone for personal communications devices, and commercial travel for video "transporters." It is here that the appetite for "more, better, faster" is insatiable and the growth in demand for the same is unstoppable.

CHAPTER FOUR

Standards, Services, and Equipment

A standard is a set of principles that describe the vocabulary, design, operation, maintenance, and inter-operability of a device or system intended for widespread use throughout an industry. The standard can be for a new product or service, such as ATM, or to recognize and elevate widely used and accepted industry-developed devices or systems (*de facto* standards) to standard status.

ATM Standards Organization

The International Telecommunications Union (ITU), a specialized agency of the United Nations, with headquarters in Geneva, Switzerland, is comprised of membership from more than 150 nations. The mission of the ITU is to regulate the international use of, and foster development in, telecommunications. Delegates represent the interests of their country's network operations and administration.

One long-term goal of the ITU has been the development of a set of standards for an Integrated Broadband Communications Network (IBCN). Within this organization, scientific and technical studies are prepared by standing committees, who work with and coordinate the activities of work/study groups from the member nations. External organizations, such as Research on Advanced

Communications in Europe (RACE), Institute of Electrical and Electronics Engineers (IEEE), Bell Communications Research (Bell Core), and many university centers, provide personnel and research time toward the standardization effort. The intent of this participation is essentially to ensure that the very best thinking is applied to the standards and that each member nation can place emphasis on what is important to their nation's segment of the industry, e.g., real time or bursty services.

Groups of manufacturers, providers, and users, such as the ATM Forum, organize to further the standards activity within their member nations. Regarding the ATM Forum, their focus on ATM standards differ from the ITU. Where the ITU's activities are analogous to a "top down" approach, the ATM Forum favors the "bottom up" approach, reflecting the needs of the user and the Customer Premises Equipment (CPE) manufacturers. While at first this dichotomy may appear contentious, designer goals and user needs must be aligned in order to accelerate the development and deployment of ATM products and services. To that end, the ATM Forum has performed very well. Formed in October of 1991, their first specifications for public and private network interfaces were released in June of 1992, coinciding with the ITU's ATM Recommendations in the same month. In large part the ATM Forum's activities helped to initiate the first commercial ATM service, in August 1993. Since the June 1992 announcement, the ATM Forum has continued its work toward additional specifications, such as signaling and congestion control.

This brief definition and summary of the standards organization will be useful in the following discussion of the principles developed by and for ATM. It is important to understand that, in a large international organization, a great deal of cooperation is necessary to reach an accord. To a certain extent, it can be inferred from Chapter 2 that both technical argument and compromise have been shown as parallel avenues toward acceptance in standards development. Furthermore, it should be understood that a standard is not static. Variations, or options, exist, some of which may see limited application; others are constantly being evaluated and may be modified as ATM technology and network equipment evolves. Differences between standards and current implementations will be discussed in subsequent chapters, or where it seems most appropriate. A list of ITU

Recommendations and ATM Forum Specifications is included as an Appendix for the reader's use.

The Transfer Mode

Asynchronous Transfer Mode (ATM) is a connection-oriented switching and asynchronous multiplexing methodology transporting fixed-length cells. The word *asynchronous* refers, in part, to the untimed relationship between the sender and the receiver. Being a packet oriented technology, the cell (packet) has an information field for data and a header for identifying and routing the cell. Transport speeds are possible at 2.4 Gigabit rates and higher. Introductory rates of 1.544 and 45 Megabits are commercially available today, with 155 Megabits-per-second service available on an individual case basis (see Figure 4.1).

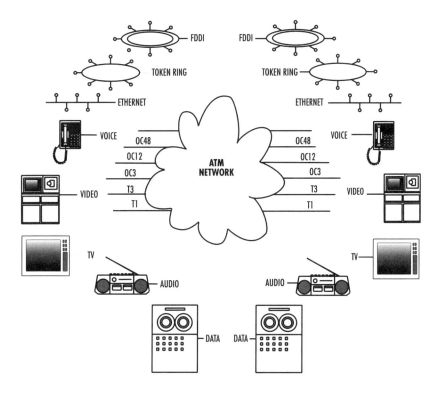

Figure 4.1 The ATM network concept.

The cell is specific to ATM in that the information field is transported transparently across the network. No error control is exerted upon the information field in the network. Furthermore, the flexibility of ATM permits connection-oriented (e.g. voice, video) and connectionless (e.g., LAN) traffic to be mixed in the same system. The individual requirements are accommodated in the ATM Adaptation Layer (AAL) where the application-specific parameters, such as delay and loss recovery, are embedded in the information field. This allows the network to adapt to the application, contrary to conventional transport modes.

Cell Structure

The ATM cell is 53 bytes in length. Forty-eight octets are used for the information field, the remaining five octets comprise the header. The information field, as explained above, is transported from sender to receiver with no corrective or protective action taken by the network. The code embedded in the information field, by the ATM Adaptation Layer (AAL), is interpreted by the receiving station's AAL.

The header uses its 40 bits to set up routing, cell identity, and error control (Figure 4.2). Routing for the cell is determined by the Virtual Channel Identifier (VCI) and the Virtual Path Identifier (VPI). The term virtual (or semi-permanent) is used because the resources are assigned only during the time required to carry a given message.

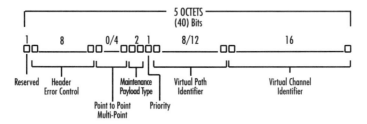

Figure 4.2 Conceptual ATM header structure.

Virtual Identifiers

Within the physical loop to the user, ATM provides end-to-end connectivity by means of logical channels, similar to packet switching.

For greater flexibility, ATM uses a two-level hierarchy for routing, which yields the virtual path and the virtual channel identities. The virtual path identifier describes the semi-permanent route between two end points. The variation in the VPI bit field (8 or 12 bits) allows from 256 to 4096 paths to be identified.

The virtual channel identifier describes a cell transmission channel inside the virtual path. A virtual channel provides the connection between a sender and receiver. Thousands of channels can be identified in each virtual path. Each channel transports independently of all other channels, which allows the same path to carry all information types, e.g., voice, data, and video. Consider this independence in a conference application. By using ATM, bandwidth is available on demand, instead of a conventional arrangement where reserved bandwidth is decided in advance of the conference. With ATM, the video could use channel 1, voice on channel 2, and, if needed, data could be transported on channel 3. Resources are only used when information is actually sent. In the public network, the ATM solution provides the flexibility to make dynamic decisions during the conference, for example, "send data now", and resource cost would be based on use, not the prearranged bandwidth. There would be advantages for private networks as well since limited network resources would not be set aside or restricted to a conference application.

Priorities

A priority or Quality of Service (QOS) marker in the header allows the ATM network to recognize differences in the traffic types in terms of cell loss, delay, and jitter delay. This refers to the semantic transparency (cell loss) and time transparency (delay) discussed in Chapter 2. Each traffic type has different tolerances to cell loss and delay and the Priority Identifier (PI) is used to show these differences. PI, or QOS, can be identified on the basis of per cell, channel, or path. Multiple service classes are provided, which ensures the appropriate handling of all traffic. PI also permits the ATM network to adjust traffic at times of overload.

Payload

The information field is normally carried transparently across the network. The network, though, must be maintained and monitored in order to maximize its usefulness, The *Payload Type Identifier* (PTI) is used to distinguish network maintenance messaging from normal traffic. A maintenance message is a special cell which can be inserted and extracted at specific points within the network on a virtual channel basis. The links, multiplexers, and switches, for example, can be individually checked for performance with this technique.

Access

An important distinction for the ATM network is whether the connection is to be point-to-point or point-to-multipoint. When users have a predefined signaling channel, they will be permitted to instantaneously request the desired logical connections needed. These connections, Switched Virtual Connections (SVC), will set up the desired single or multipoint access. Until that signaling protocol is defined and implemented, logical connectivity is predefined by using Permanent Virtual Channels (PVC), which can satisfy point-to-point and point-to-multipoint applications.

Error Control

Network-based error control is limited to the header only. In the ATM network, Header Error Control (HEC) is used to correct single bit header errors and detect burst errors. It is important to the sharing of a broadband network's resources that easily corrected errors not be allowed to multiply their individual effect across the network. This protocol looks to detect single bit errors and corrects them. A bit error in the header could inadvertently corrupt one cell's VPI/VCI to a legitimate value of another user, resulting in misrouting. Burst errors which affect the header will logically corrupt more than one bit, perhaps the information bits as well, even multiple cells.

When an error is found in cell A, for example, the correction process fixes the error, then sets the protocol to detection. The single error is corrected and cell A is sent on its way (Figure 4.3a). But if this error were the result of a burst error, only the first error in cell A would be corrected. This cell would be sent, probably misrouted. However, the detection process would see errors in subsequent cells B, C, D, etc., discarding each header with errors. With the first error-free header, cell E, the protocol resets to error correction (Figure 4.3b).

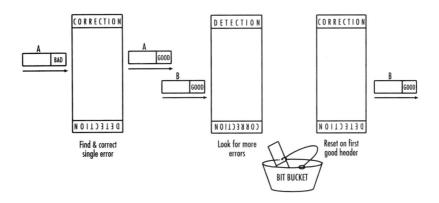

Figure 4.3a. Bit error correction and reset.

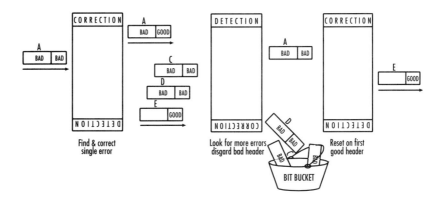

Figure 4.3b. Burst error correction and reset.

Reserve

One bit is left in the header, reserved for future use. This may seem like a rather small quantity at first. Upon reflection though, the balance of the header information appears to cover all the bases. Possible uses for the reserved bit could be to modify existing header fields, synchronization, modify information field data, encryption, etc.

Routing and Resources

Routing information is embedded in the header, as discussed above. The VPI and VCI define the path and channel to be used for the information transfer. ATM is a connection-oriented service, requiring the network to determine, in advance of establishing a connection, that sufficient resources are available, in terms of links, queues, switches, and multiplexers. But it is not *just* the availability of resources, but resources *sufficient* for the bandwidth and the priority requested that are essential to that determination. When the signaling protocol is fully established, a signaling channel will allow negotiations with the network, where a user may be willing to degrade quality for transport capacity *before* setup, and later, during the transmission, to upgrade quality when the necessary resources become available.

Information Rate and Control

There are differences between the International Telecommunications Union's (ITU) principles and those of the ATM Forum. It is interesting to note that in the June 1992 Recommendations, the ITU only standardized the Peak Cell Rate (PCR) as a throughput parameter. The decision for other parameters was left to further study due to concerns of resource access, sharing, and bandwidth savings. The ATM Forum introduced the concept of the Sustainable Cell Rate (SCR) as an optional traffic management parameter to define the minimum information rate allowed. This decision was perhaps more philosophical than technical since the SCR minimum does not prevent the ATM Forum from the use of PCR as the maximum.

A shared broadband network with the Asynchronous Transfer Mode attempts to transport, while minimizing cell loss, information up to the physical cell limit of the medium. Because the network is shared, it is necessary to detect accidental or intentional abuse of the user's agreed throughput. The ITU would seek to police on the basis of peak cell rate as a usage control parameter. Theoretically, the ATM Forum polices on a maximum (PCR) rate as well. In the initial ATM network offering, an information rate is set per Permanent Virtual Channel (PVC), in increments of, for example, 64,000 bits per second or 1,000,000 bits per second. Conforming traffic, at or below the agreed information rate, is permitted into the network at the ingress port of the ATM switch. The ingress port will discard nonconforming traffic, i.e., rates that exceed the agreed information rate.

Signaling and Flow Control

A reference made earlier indicated that a signaling protocol is not fully developed, although delivery is expected within a year. A separate signaling virtual channel will be used to allow network access for transport negotiations, based on the enhanced signaling concepts of Narrowband Integrated Services Digital Network (NISDN). The ATM Forum has specified limited signaling initiatives at the outset. The improved signal protocol will, among other features, provide a choice between today's PVC, with fixed parameters, and a switched virtual channel (SVC), dynamically allocated, negotiable, and with logical permanence.

One of the principles of ATM is to keep the network simple and to maximize network utilization. To that end, flow control has been discussed as a "boundary" option, to be performed once at the edge of the network and not inside the network. A General Flow Control (GFC) procedure has been proposed at the User Network Interface (UNI) for some situations involving point-to-multipoint configurations. As ATM technology advances from PVC connections, the GFC protocol will become a more meaningful parameter.

Protocol Reference Model

The ITU has defined a layered model similar to an Open Systems Interconnection (OSI) logical hierarchical architecture, consisting of three layers and several sublayers. Figure 4.4 shows the architectural structure. The sublayers and their functions will be illustrated in their respective sections. Appropriate specifications have been adopted by both the ITU and the ATM Forum for each of these layers.

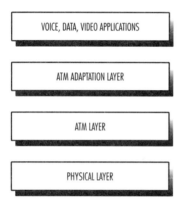

Figure 4.4. ATM logical architecture.

Physical Layer

The physical layer converts the cell stream into transportable bits and supports the physical medium bit functions (Figure 4.5a). At its lowest sublayer, Physical Medium (PM), the interface is electrically or optically medium-dependent. In the upper layer, Transmission Convergence (TC), the transmitter's and receiver's peer relationship guarantee bit timing and line coding, insertion and reconstruction, respectively. Four types of frame adaptation are specified in the Transmission Convergence Sublayer, Synchronous Digital Hierarchy (SDH), Plesiochronous Digital Hierarchy (PDH), cell-based adaptations and the fourth, added by the ATM Forum, the Fiber Distributed Data Interface (FDDI) option for private networks.

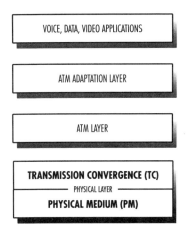

Figure 4.5a. ATM physical layer sublayers.

The physical medium can be electrical or optical, fiber being the preferred medium. Medium transmission rates are 155.520 Megabits, and 622.080 Megabits on single mode fiber only. Information rates available for SDH and the cell-based option are 149.760 Megabits at 155 Megabits and 599.040 Megabits at 622 Megabits. The ATM Forum specifies a Synchronous Optical NETwork (SONET) interface for both public and private SDH implementations. The ITU's SDH and SONET are not identical specifications, but they are compatible at 155 and 622 Megabits and 2.5 Gigabits. Only private interfaces are specified for the cell-based option.

The Plesiochronous Digital Hierarchy (PDH) option for mapping ATM cells can take advantage of existing network equipment, which the ATM Forum sees as a more expedient process for introducing ATM services. Basing ATM on the current DS3 for the public interface, and using the Physical Layer Convergence Protocol (PLCP) the information rate is set at 40.704 Megabits. The ITU approach for PDH is more SDH-like in framing and delineation, giving 34.368 Megabits. As a point of interest, a very recent service offering of T1 ATM service uses ITU's HEC mapping scheme giving the user a 1.39 Megabit information rate on a T1 access link, as opposed to the PLCP rate of 1.17 Megabits.

The ATM Forum's private interface for multimode fiber is based on the FDDI physical layer, giving a 100 Megabit information rate.

ATM Layer

Completing the ATM cell structure and setting up the cell streams for transmission of outgoing traffic, and the reverse process for incoming, are the major functions performed in this layer (Figure 4.5b). The preset values of the five octet header, added to the 48 octet information field, are loaded with the necessary identifiers, previously discussed. The ATM Forum's specifications differ from the preset values in several ways, such as giving this layer use of all payload and cell loss fields and introducing the Interim Local Management Interface (ILMI). ILMI provides the ATM device with status and configuration information on path and channel availability at its User Network Interface (UNI) in the absence of local network management procedures.

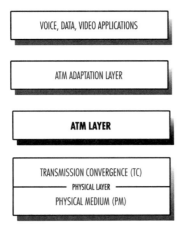

Figure 4.5b. ATM layer.

ATM Adaptation Layer

The Adaptation Layer is service-specific, mapping the control, management and user Protocol Data Units (PDU) into cells, and building PDUs from incoming cells (Figure 4.5c). Some of the detail involved is time stamping and recovery for isochronous information, bit error and cell-loss monitoring and corrective actions, and cell payload assembly delay control. The sequence information from the Convergence Sublayer (CS) is contained in the SAR-PDU octet, added to the 47 octet SAR-PDU payload to form the 48 octet cell.

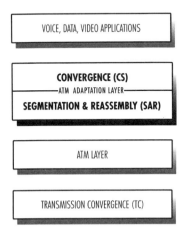

Figure 4.5c. ATM adaptation layer sublayers.

Service-specific issues are connection mode, bit rate, and delay sensitivity. From combinations of the three parameters, four classifications are developed which fit today's services, leading to four types of ATM adaptation layer (AAL) protocols (Figure 4.6).

AAL TYPE	CLASS	TIMING	BIT RATE	CONNECTION MODE ORIENTATION
1	A	Required	Constant	Connection
2	B	Required	Variable	Connection
3/4, 5	C	Not Required	Variable	Connection
3/4	D	Not Required	Variable	Connectionless

Figure 4.6. ATM adaptation layer protocol types.

AAL 1 is designed for Constant Bit Rate (CBR) traffic, which is sensitive to delay and cell loss. Voice and video services require this protocol type to insure delivery and recovery of the constant bit source, timing and loss indicators, e.g., convergence sublayer (CS) sequence number. The sequence number can be used to detect loss and misinsertion of SAR payloads. The CS layer specifically addresses all delay, e.g., jitter and assembly delay. The CS layer is also responsible for time stamp insertion and recovery.

AAL 2 is similar to AAL 1, except that AAL 2 is for Variable Bit Rate (VBR) service. With a VBR, the cell fill level may vary between cells. This variation will force the SAR toward greater functionality. Time and cell loss sensitivity require the CS to perform time stamp recovery to track sequence numbering as in AAL 1, and to direct recovery procedures for audio and video services.

AAL 3/4 serves both connection-oriented and connectionless traffic in either the message or streaming modes. Although all connectionless functions are not provided for, the Multiplexing IDentifier (MID), in the CS-PDU, allows a connectionless server in a Local Area Network (LAN) to identify the originating/destination device.

AAL 5, as specified by the ATM Forum, offers better service to high speed, connection-oriented data users by reducing overhead and improving error protection. AAL 5 functions in the same manner as AAL 3/4 with exceptions noted in multiplexing, error detection, and peer-to-peer buffer allocation indicators. The ITU has begun looking at AAL 5 for Class C services. The ATM Forum has also specified AAL 5 for signaling between the User Network Interface (UNI) and the Network Node Interface (NNI).

Operations and Maintenance

Performance monitoring, failure detection, system protection, event reporting, and fault isolation are the major parameters determined useful in a broadband network. The intent is to maximize network operation and minimize physical maintenance activities. This controlled maintenance concept organizes the Operations And Maintenance (OAM) functions in a layered pattern (Figure 4.7), corresponding to the Protocol Reference Model (PRM).

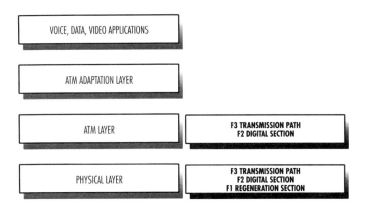

Figure 4.7. OAM relationship to physical reference model.

The concept of a reference model management function, the relationship of the OAM levels to the five transmission options, and the applicable AAL are *not* shown in Figure 4.7. This information can be found in the OAM recommendations as they evolve with the ATM technology. Not all levels will be found in all locations across the network, nor do all levels interact between layers. It will better serve the prospective user to get detailed, service-specific OAM information from prospective providers and vendors.

ATM Services and Customer Premises Equipment

Vendor products and network services for ATM networks, premises-based, public, and private networks, have been available from a variety of sources since the first commercial introduction in 1993. Most of the major Interexchange Carriers (IXC) have an ATM offering or have released a delivery schedule. At this juncture, the Local Exchange Carriers (LEC), or local telephone companies, have not introduced a commercially available ATM service. One or more of the IXCs may, for a short duration, be offering a nonstandard or quasi-ATM. The ability to make any offering depends heavily on the provider's current network structure, successful beta-testing, and their ability to properly position their offering to, and successfully implement ATM for, their clients.

There are a wide variety of products and services being introduced for ATM networks and users. The next section is intended to generically list provider and vendor offerings. Where certain language or terms may appear vendor- or provider-specific, it is not with the intent to specify any one provider or vendor.

Introduction schedules will differ across the board, but for our purposes, this discussion will look at six elements which seem to be a practical set of deliverables. In all cases of service availability listed below, switches, multiplexers, and routers are compatible with the ATM Forum's current specifications, such as the customer premises equipment's (CPE) compliance with User Network Interface (UNI) v3.1.

Service Introduction

The six elements used for descriptive purposes are:

- Access
- Connection
- Service Class
- Information Rate
- Management
- Customer Premises Equipment (CPE)

A typical provider schedule may list their beta-testing and order acceptance dates. Many vendors will have CPE available to match the provider's time frame. Expect order intervals to range from 30 to 180 days, depending on the provider, vendor, and the type(s) of access required.

ACCESS

T3/OC3

T3 ATM access will be on an unchanneled 45 Megabit facility provisioned by the service provider or the user. OC3c ATM access (optical carrier) will be at 155 Megabits. OC3c access may depend on the availability of SONET and local exchange carrier (LEC) SONET presence. For some period of time it should be expected that OC3c access will be treated on an individual case basis.

T3/OC3c ATM access will place a T3/OC3 ATM Data Service Unit/Multiplexer (DSU/MUX) on the user's premises. A router will send data to the DSU/MUX using ATM Digital Exchange Interface (DXI) protocol over V.35, RS449, or High Speed Serial Interface (HSSI). HSSI will permit the highest data rate for T3 access. The DSU/MUX will adapt data traffic to ATM cells using ATM Adaptation Layer (AAL) 3/4 or AAL 5, and map the traffic to the T3/OC3c facility. The DSU/MUX will also accept isochronous Private Branch Exchange (PBX) using DSX-1 protocol, and video conferencing using V.35. In both cases, the voice and video, DSU/MUX adapts the traffic to cells and maps the cells with AAL 1. Figure 4.8 lets you look inside the ATM cloud to view the T3/OC3 ATM network.

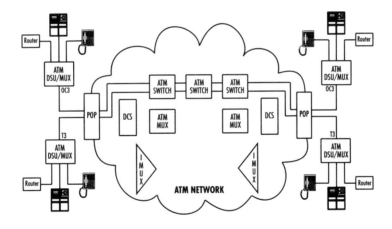

Figure 4.8. T3 and OC3 ATM access.

T1

T1 ATM access provides 1.544 megabit service with the access facility provisioned by the user or the provider. This recently announced access offering will be instrumental in making ATM services a reality for many users whose needs are less massive. The DSU/MUX will accept voice, video, and data inputs for transport on a single facility in a manner similar to the T3 access. The DXI protocol, over a V.35 or RS449 interface, is available and the DSU/MUX uses AAL 3/4 or AAL 5 for data and AAL 1 for voice and video. Figure 4.9 depicts the T1 ATM Network, with T1 end-to-end service.

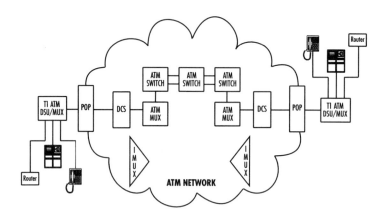

Figure 4.9. T1 ATM access.

T1 Emulation

T1 circuit emulation access provides network ingress to a T3 ATM network, where an existing Time Division Multiplexer (TDM) is in place, protecting a user's equipment investment, and allowing low-volume locations to share the use of the larger backbone circuit. Some restrictions may apply, such as traffic delivery to one location only, all emulation input being treated as low-speed AAL 1 traffic. Translations at the destination are returned to T1 framing, with delivery at the destination via a TDM (Figure 4.10).

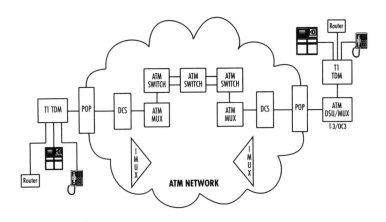

Figure 4.10. T1 emulation ATM access.

Multiple T1

Multiple T1 access allows an aggregate of bandwidth to be available for data and Variable Bit Rate (VBR) applications. Unchanneled T1s, user- or provider-provisioned, would interface to an Inverse Multiplexer (IMUX). Traffic from the information source is then routed to the IMUX using ATM DXI over V.35, RS449, or HSSI where the traffic is treated as one data stream across the multiple T1s. Restrictions of the CPE may require limits on the minimum and maximum of T1s permitted and the multiples that may be added. For example, one vendor's equipment requires two T1 multiples up to a maximum of eight T1s. Available bandwidth in this situation would range from 3.12 to 12.352 Megabits. Also, current CPE used with this service access does not support ATM functions, simply carrying ATM DXI protocols transparently. At the ATM MUX, inside the network, traffic is adapted to cells and mapped using AAL 5. Figure 4.11 shows two implementations of this access.

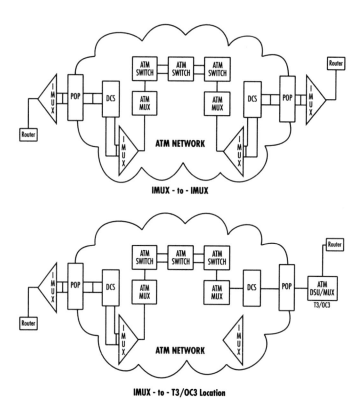

Figure 4.11. Multiple T1 ATM access.

Frame Relay

Frame relay access sets up an internetworking relationship between frame relay services and ATM networks following the Frame Relay Forum's Frame Relay/ATM PVC Service Implementation Agreement FRF.8. For a user with multiple 56/64 Kilobit (DS0) and T1 Frame Relay (FR) services, a provider would convert one site to T3 ATM access (Figure 4.12). This FR/ATM interface becomes the location for all ATM and Frame Relay users to be logically internetworked. The ATM site performs no FR functions and the FR sites do not execute ATM functions. Specific internetworking functions, such as translating higher-layer multi-protocol encapsulation procedures for end system requirements, are based on the International Telecommunications

Union-Telecommunications Sector (ITU-T) I.555 Recommendations. These are performed in the provider's gateway. Multiprotocol encapsulation procedures involve ATM DXI Lower Layer Compatibility (LLC for ISDN), Logical Link Control (LLC for LAN)/Sub-Network Access Protocol (SNAP) to and from FR's Network Layer Protocol IDentifier (NLPID)/SNAP.

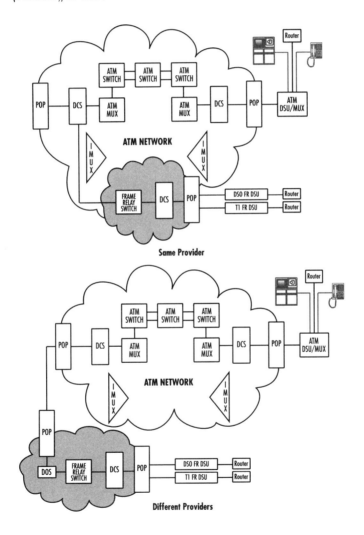

Figure 4.12. Frame Relay ATM access.

The network-based ATM MUX executes the AAL 5 protocol, establishing the cell and mapping the Data Link Control Identifier (DLCI) into the VPI/VCI address, then mapping the cell on to the FR-T1 ATM link with other FR traffic.

TCP/IP

Transmission Control Protocol/Internet Protocol (TCP/IP) access provides internetworking with ATM users and ingress to the Global Internet. A CPE router equipped with a T3 ATM Interface Processor (AIP) will use AAL 5 for encapsulation and mapping of the IP datagram to ATM cell traffic then onto the ATM network (Figure 4.13). The same protocol encapsulation, described above, is required for LLC/SNAP. AIP licensing agreements will increase the number of CPE manufacturer's routers with this capacity. For some time, there may be limited numbers of vendor's products with this capability.

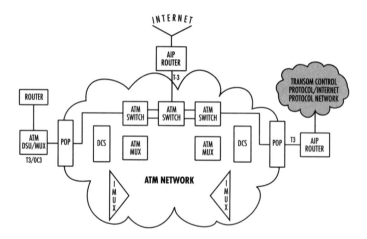

Figure 4.13. TCP/IP ATM access.

Restrictions may limit information rates, but you may expect to find providers who can offer 64, 128, 384, and 512 Kilobit rates. Also, IP address and domain name registrations are applicable, in accordance with Internet Activities Board (IAB) guidelines.

Other Access

As an emerging technology, ATM access is not yet fully mature. From previous references, it can be seen that some limitations exist for voice and video interfaces. SONET access is also incomplete for the present. It is expected that, at a minimum, an international gateway and a local exchange carrier (LEC) ATM Interconnect, based on LEC SONET implementations, will be provisioned by all providers in the future.

CONNECTION

An ATM network is connection-oriented, setting up a logical two-way circuit between the end users. Permanent virtual connections and switched virtual connections have been discussed previously. Initial offerings of PVCs will still use the virtual path identifier (VPI) and virtual channel identifier (VCI) addresses in the cell header for routing across the ATM network. The VPI/VCI addresses are reused on each physical interface, uniquely identifying a virtual channel (VC).

PVCs are bi-directional and asymmetrical, i.e., traffic flows in both directions, and the information rate can be higher in one direction. PVCs can be configured as virtual path connections and virtual channel connections. The virtual path connection identifies a sequence of Virtual Path (VP) segments making an end-to-end connection. A VP may consist of many virtual channel connections. A virtual channel connection identifies a sequence of Virtual Channel (VC) segments connecting two ATM-communicating entities. Figure 4.14 illustrates these logical connections.

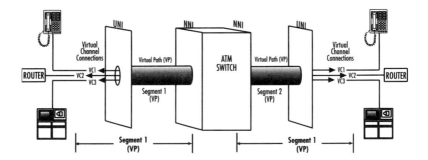

Figure 4.14. ATM logical connections.

PVCs can be ordered as virtual path connection-based, for example, with the provider provisioning and maintaining a single VPC, while the user administers their own VCs within. The provider may assign all PVI and VCI addresses being used with the PVC access.

SERVICE CLASS

Each PVC will be assigned a Class of Service (COS), which will define the service parameters needed to satisfy the unique requirements of the application using that PVC. The COS of a VPC will be set at the level of the most stringent VC. Examples of the COS are Constant Bit Rate (CBR) and Variable Bit Rate (VBR). CBR is intended for time-sensitive, isochronous traffic such as video, while VBR is more delay-independent and satisfies bursty data traffic.

INFORMATION RATE

The maximum information rate is the *Peak Cell Rate* (PCR). Again, as mentioned previously, traffic is bi-directional and the information rate can be asymmetric. The PCR may be specified as the maximum limit per VCC or VPC. Information rates are assignable to each Class of Service assigned. Minimum information rates of 64 Kilobits, 1 Megabit, and 1.544 Megabits, for T1 emulation, can be expected. The ATM Forum has specified an optional traffic management parameter, the Sustainable Cell Rate (SCR) parameter, in the User Network Interface (UNI). The SCR defines the minimum information rate allowed per PVC. The ingress port on the ATM switch polices the assigned information rate, passing conforming rates and discarding nonconforming rates.

It should be noted that providers may offer a variation called the Committed Information Rate (CIR), a term associated with some frame relay services. The CIR is used in the same way as the SCR defined by the ATM Forum. At least one provider has used the CIR terminology to set the access CIR to zero, meaning the committed, or minimum, rate is zero bits per second. The access channel speed is used as the maximum access rate. The PCR is the maximum rate in the ATM network. This methodology reduces cell loss where a public network access link transmits at the SCR. An information burst at the access line rate, e.g., 64 Kilobits may exceed the SCR which can be less than the access link speed, causing cell loss.

MANAGEMENT

An enhancement to the initial ATM offering is the planned implementation of Simple Network Management Protocol (SNMP). To the user, the ATM network will appear as a SNMP agent. Network events identified by the user will be exported, via ATM Proxy Agent Management Information Bases (MIB), on a separate circuit in "near" real time. The circuit will connect the ATM network's Management System (MS) host to the user MIB. Access information will be for each switch and multiplexer where event alarms and messages can report on T3 trunks and the ATM layers. Privacy and security are assured by host partitioning and through access verification of SNMP community name, string, and IP address. Among the first introductions are a basic management package for automatic delivery of network alarms and an advanced offering giving users the ability to request configuration, performance, and administrative information for their ATM network.

CUSTOMER PREMISES EQUIPMENT (CPE)

Four major types of CPE are available for the current offerings of ATM networking. These are:

- Access
- Routers
- ATM Local Area Network Switches
- Private Wide Area Network Switches

Specific CPE is leased or sold, installed, and maintained by the ATM provider. Other CPE is possible where a provider has a certification program to certify other manufacturer's CPE. With a certification program in place, providers will have CPE already in the process, as manufacturers submit their products, in advance of user demand.

Access

These products include the Digital Service Unit/Customer Service Unit (DSU/CSU) access multiplexers and the DSU/MUXs for connecting the user source, Data Terminal Equipment (DTE), to the ATM access link.

Single-port and multiport devices are available with V.35 and HSSI interfaces.

Routers

A router provides multi-protocol internetworking on ATM networks. An early implementation placed a DSU with ATM functionality between the router and the ATM network. The interface was HSSI with DXI protocol. The DSU performed segmentation and reassembly, to and from the cell. Now advanced routers offer an ATM Interface Processor (AIP), discussed previously, i.e., TCP/IP. Interface speeds are planned to increase to OC12 (622.08 Gigabits).

Models with integrated ATM AAL 5 capability, will be performing the multiprotocol encapsulation discussed above. Expectations are for multimode interfaces to be introduced for both Local Area Networks (LAN) and Wide Area Networks (WAN) applications at 100 and 155 Megabits. Single mode fiber will have an interface at SONET OC3c speeds (155.52 Megabits).

LAN Switch

The ATM LAN switch provides PVC trunking and native mode LAN connections. This is a powerful merging of LAN and ATM technologies that will impact the user community with high capacity routers and perhaps the next generation of wiring hubs. One manufacturer's vision sees the use of this combined technology giving the functionality of a single router across an entire network, in a virtually seamless manner.

Large campus environments and multimedia-dependent applications, for example, will not suffer from network interface bottlenecks as ATM switching fabrics are placed on the boundary of the network, bringing ATM network transmission rates across the curb, to the user's doorstep. User Network Interface (UNI) speeds of OC12 (622.08 Megabits) may soon be replaced with OC48 (2.5 Gigabits) and perhaps eventually with OC96 (5 Gigabits).

Available technology offers modular designs with up to 2.5 Gigabit aggregate bandwidth, and larger platforms featuring a 10 Gigabit nonblocking architecture.

PrivateWAN Switch

This unit is used as the main switch in a private or hybrid network. Initial offerings included blocking or non-blocking architectures. Platforms are ATM cell switching or a combined ATM and adaptation switching for non-ATM interfaces. Interfaces are T1, T3, OC3, Ethernet, video, single- and multimode fiber, and Frame Relay. Later releases added UNI/NNI features, token ring, and FDDI interfaces.

Adaptation services include VP support and PCR policing per VP/VC, AAL 1, 3/4, and 5 capabilities and a wide variety of interface protocols. Switching fabrics range from 3.2 Gigabits to 12.8 Gigabits.

Quality Objectives

The ATM Forum has specified quality objectives which a user can expect from ATM network providers. Some providers are making a point of showing how they exceed these specifications, and in doing so are establishing a level of differentiation for their services. Quality objectives are usually grouped under three categories: performance, service, and provisioning. Measurements based on the provider's Point of Presence (POP) to POP domain and end-to-end (UNI to UNI) system giving a complete picture of the quality of service provided.

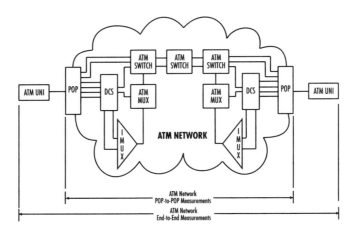

Figure 4.15. Quality measurement reference.

PERFORMANCE

Measurements would include various cell parameters based on the domain measured and the class of service, i.e., continuous bit rate (CBR) or variable bit rate (VBR). The parameters measured would be delay, jitter, error, loss, and misinsertion.

Quality Measurement	Variable Bit Rate Class of Service				Continuous Bit Rate Class of Service			
	Objective POP to POP	Actual POP to POP	Objective End to End	Actual End to End	Objective POP to POP	Actual POP to POP	Objective End to End	Actual End to End
DELAY								
JITTER DELAY								
CELL ERROR RATIOS								
CELL LOSS RATIOS								
MISINSERTION RATES								

Figure 4.16. Charting performance measurements.

SERVICE

This category contains subjective and objective measurements, such as service hours, service availability, Mean Time To Repair (MTTR) and Mean Time To Service Restorable (MTTSR). MTTSR would be measured over time, involving several events, in order to determine a realistic average. MTTR is usually prioritized, from priority 1 to priority n, in either ascending or descending criticality, based on the nature of the event.

SERVICE	POP to POP			END to END		
Availability	Objective	Time In Service	% Available	Objective	Time In Service	% Available
MTTSR	# of Events	Total Hours	Avg. Restoral Time	# of Events	Total Hours	Avg. Restoral Time
MTTSR Priority 1 (highest)	Objective	Actual	Mean Time	Objective	Actual	Mean Time
Priority n (lowest)						

Figure 4.17. Charting service measurements.

PROVISIONING

Statistically, this measurement can be made objective, but in reality there is more subjectivity inherent in the measurement due to human factors. Provisioning objectives are often met and surpassed as implementations and post-implementation functions proceed without a hitch. More praise should be heaped upon the everyday providers doing their "job" and getting "it" done.

However, users know of and remember all too well the nightmarish implementations, the pre- and post-traumas and finger pointing that seem to characterize the provisioning landscape. These occasions happen with well-entrenched technologies. What can the user expect when the technology is new and the personnel green?

Planning, coordination, and tracking, as well as expertise and experience, are the strong suits brought to the table by the provider's ATM provisioning groups. ATM may be a new technology, but to the provider's people, specialized training and on-the-job experience in large, complex implementations have left few surprises in the provisioning process. Errors may occur, and some commitments may be missed however, the processes can be completed in a competent professional manner.

Summary

This chapter has cleared away the smoke in the typical network cloud to show users, and prospective users, the structural components of this important new technology (Figure 4.18). Asynchronous Transfer Mode (ATM) is here and making a steady advance toward the goal of an Integrated Broadband Communications Network (IBCN).

Providers and manufacturers alike share the enthusiasm for the new services and products introduced as a result of ATM's emergence. Users are seeing for the first time an internetworking service whose transmission transparency is truly applications independent. Companies and organizations relying on rapid and efficient information flow as a key strategic asset will seek internetworking solutions that enhance productivity and provide competitive advantages. It seems clear that, with the evolution of the technology and the increasing awareness of its capabilities, ATM will be in service or indelibly inked into every user's information system strategy.

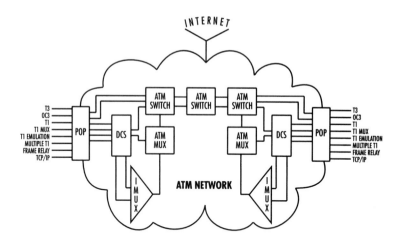

Figure 4.18. International Broadband Communications Network backbone.

CHAPTER FIVE

The ATM Backbone

Developing a high-speed multi-purpose network, such as ATM, is a cooperative effort involving several disciplines. Theorists and practitioners joined forces to give shape and substance to the elements necessary in a complete architecture. It has taken many years of collaborative effort in transmission, coding, switching, and queuing systems design to arrive at a final set of recommendations for this networking methodology. Computer models, test beds, and trial sites were set up. Simulation and actual performance and behaviors were monitored and charted. Scientific, geo-political and economic arguments, compromises and decisions culminated in what is now known as Asynchronous Transfer Mode.

Backbone Nomenclature

Asynchronous Transfer Mode is the name given to the set of principles that govern the physical structure and the operational characteristics of this new integrated broadband network. The elements of this network, the transmission and switching components, are the physical manifestations of the completed design. These elements comprise the major skeletal structure of the network, giving form to the architecture and supporting the interconnection for the extremities that serve as the user's interface.

From this anatomical analogy we can aptly refer to the ATM network as the backbone of a communications architecture. Specific transmission, switching, and multiplexing elements form the ATM backbone. It is useful to understand the network's backbone elements for making informed decisions regarding the anticipated values stemming from the implementation of an ATM network. In previous chapters we have discussed these elements, and several components, such as queuing and translations. In this chapter we will look again at switching and multiplexing, but the focus will be on the transmission element, optical fiber.

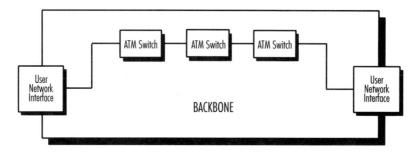

Figure 5.1 The network backbone.

The Transmission System

Optical fiber is the preferred transmission medium in an ATM network. Many decisions which affect such principles as queuing and error ratios, are predicated on the use of this technically clean, high-speed medium. However, optical fiber was playing an important role in telecommunications several years in advance of the ATM standard.

The public telephone network began as an analog communications system optimized for the transmission of voice conversations. For nearly a century, there was no impetus for change. The network itself had been upgraded and improved several times, primarily in

switching and multiplexing capabilities, but the dominant application for the network was voice. Through the early years of data
transmission, the use of modems and line conditioning permitted
the public network to adapt other signal types to be converted for
effective transmission in a pure analog or quasi-analog format.
Analog carrier systems, i.e., copper wire cable, coaxial cable, and
microwave-based, provided the means to respond to increased traffic
demands by multiplexing many users onto a single facility.
Overhead and underground cable congestion issues were reduced by
these systems, in both local and long-distance facility routes.

Figure 5.2 Overhead cable distribution, early 1900s.
(Source: *100 Years of New Beginnings*, Bell of Pennsylvania)

Traffic growth and new technology were two major factors that led to
the development of digital carrier systems (see Figure 5.3). Wire
cables, microwave, and satellites systems were equipped as digital
carriers expanding the capacity of long-distance networks initially
and gradually into the local public and private networks. There were
significant improvements over the analog systems, such as reduced

noise and greatly increased capacity. Yet many problems persisted and several, such as congestion in the cable rights-of-way, would not go away.

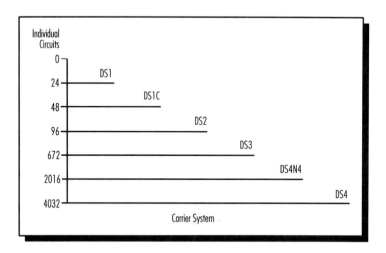

Figure 5.3 Digital carrier hierarchy.

Fiber-Optic Development

New technology and traffic growth were again catalysts in the development of fiber-optic cables and electrical-to-optical conversion equipment for use in telecommunications transmission applications. Electrical signals, i.e., data pulses, could be used to trigger the emission of light pulses into an optical cable. The light pulses could be used to re-create the original data pulses at a distant receiver (see Figure 5.4). At first the speed of the electrical-to-optical conversion equipment could not begin to approach the capacity of the optical fiber, and, because of the high costs, there was little or no discussion of the use of optical fibers in anything but the long-distance network.

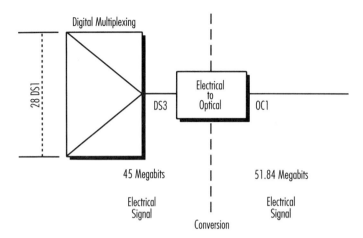

Figure 5.4 Conceptual fiber-optic transmission system.

That was barely 25 years ago. In the intervening years, declining cost, technological improvements, divestiture, and competition for a share of the telecommunications market has changed that perception forever.

With all businesses becoming more dependent on data applications, capacity and durability became more critical factors in network planning. The seemingly endless capacity of fiber optics, coupled with proven durability in long-distance networks and the profusion of optical end-user products, helped to move fiber-optic solutions "in" as the preferred choice for designers. Fiber-optic segments and complete networks are now found in nearly all sectors of business. Within the last several years, residential applications have brought fiber connectivity into private homes.

Synchronous Optical Network

In 1984, the Exchange Carriers Standards Association (ECSA) developed the Synchronous Optical Network (SONET) for the American

National Standards Institute (ANSI). SONET is designed to meet the needs of high-bandwidth applications, increased data traffic, faster speeds, improved performance and a much greater degree of survivability. SONET is the broadband networking standard in the United States. The International Telecommunications Union (ITU) has adopted SONET as its Synchronous Digital Hierarchy (SDH), and countries operating under ITU standards accept SDH as their broadband standard.

In Figure 5.5, the basic SONET rate of 51.84 Megabits, Optical Carrier 1 (OC-1), is the standard incremental rate for all higher speeds. For example, OC-3, at 155.52 Megabits is three increments of 51.84 Megabits (3 x 51.84 = 155.52). The electrical signal which is converted to an optical signal, as in OC-1, known as the Synchronous Transmission Signal-1 (STS-1), is at the same rate of 51.84 megabits. Each electrical signal at a higher speed than STS-1 is a multiple of STS-1, i.e., STS-3 at 155.52 megabits, coincident with the optical level signal rate. Also, for each OC level in Figure 5.5, the equivalent capacity of other digital rates are included along with a comparison between SONET and SDH line rates. This last column demonstrates the speed similarities that exist between the two standards.

64 Kilobits DS0	1.544 Megabits DS1	45 Megabits DS3	Optical Carrier	Line Rate (Megabits)	Synchronous Digital Hierarchy Line Rates (Megabits)
672	28	1	OC-1	51.85	—
2,016	84	3	OC-3	155.52	155.52
8,064	336	12	OC-12	622.08	622.08
32,256	1,344	48	OC-48	2,488.32	2,488.32
64,512	2,688	96	OC-96	4,976.64	4,976.64

Figure 5.5 Optical carrier hierarchy.

SONET sets a new standard for transmission of information at much higher rates than previously available. In addition to setting new standard transmission rates, SONET standardizes frame formats and provisioning protocols for Operations, Administration, and Maintenance (OAM). The transmission rates shown in the above chart match the link speeds referred to for asynchronous transfer mode in the previous chapters.

SONET Architecture

One of the principal purposes of SONET is to improve the durability and survivability of fiber-optic implementations. Initial fiber installations followed a linear route between end points. Back-up fiber may have been in the same right-of-way, creating a serious restoral problem, for example, in cases of cable cuts.

Even with the "Call Before You Dig" program, cables are frequently cut in excavation incidents. Natural and man-made disasters, such as fire, flood, and earthquake, can affect transmission links, e.g., the disastrous fire at a major switching center in Hinsdale, IL. With copper cable, depending on circumstances, a cut may sever and destroy several feet of cable. Restoral time is predicated on factors such as location, size of the cable, etc. A fiber-optic cut based on similar circumstances may involve the primary *and* the back-up cable in a linear route. And, in addition to the actual cut itself, the glass fibers may experience stress fractures several hundred feet in either direction from the cut. Restoral under such conditions may take days or weeks to complete.

Ring Structure

SONET constructs a *ring*, or closed loop architecture that can recognize a cut, or other failure, rerouting traffic before serious performance degradation occurs, or in advance of a service interruption. This "self-healing" feature is at the core of SONET's survivability. As will be discussed below, the self-healing standards dictate restoral times in the low millisecond values.

LOGICAL RING

Although the ring architecture in SONET implies a circular loop concept, some providers have implemented SONET rings in a linear design. In this situation, the SONET ring is logically implemented in a point-to-point cabling architecture. The standards for SONET are the same for every implementation; however, the network architecture and the deployment and distribution of optical cables and SONET equipment will surely affect the actual survivability and restoral time of the fiber link and the SONET-based carrier system. The number of Linear SONET implementations may be limited to specific situations where economics does not immediately lend itself to a physical ring structure. Some possible examples of linear implementations are provider to provider, or provider to an end-user location. The latter may be found in an operating telephone companies' (OTC) subscriber loop facility.

PHYSICAL RING

A true ring architecture appears to give the greatest degree of protection to both the provider and the user. In several center city and metropolitan areas the OTC and privately owned fiber-optic transport companies have placed SONET-based ring topologies in their area of operations, competing for high-speed data applications, back-up facilities, and disaster recovery options. Inter-Exchange Carriers (IXC) have been installing SONET-based ring topologies in both regional and country-wide implementations (see Figures 5.6a–c). In part, these implementations are in response to the growing demand for high-speed data transport. But, it is a reasonable conclusion that the full potential of a SONET implementation will be achieved in an integrated broadband networking methodology based on asynchronous transfer mode.

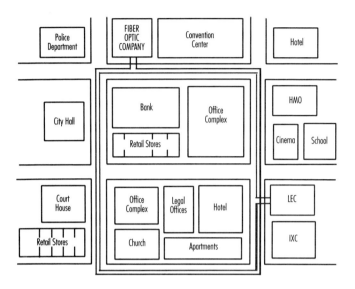

Figure 5.6a Center city ring topologies.

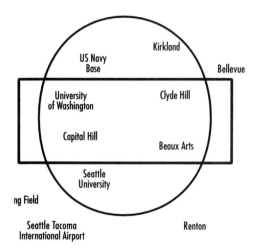

Figure 5.6b Metropolitan ring topology.

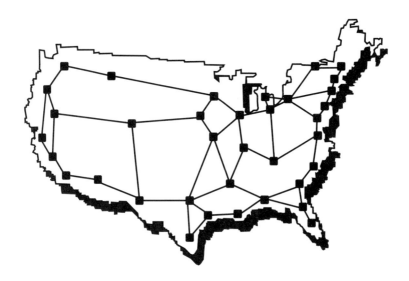

Figure 5.6c Regional and national ring topologies.

RING TYPES

SONET defines two ring types, *path-switched* and *line-switched*. Upon comparing the two types, it will appear that line-switched rings make more sense for both the user and the provider. This comparison offers several major points of difference between the types; however, other considerations, such as available traffic and economics (not discussed below), would be important factors in the implementation decision.

Path-Switched Ring

Path-switched rings require two fibers in the implementation (see Figure 5.7a). Survivability is provided for by sending all traffic in both directions on the ring. Performance is enhanced by allowing the receiving station to look at both data streams and select the better signal.

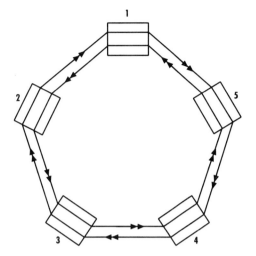

Figure 5.7a Path-switched SONET ring—normal operation.

Since the total traffic occupies both fibers, the usable transport capacity of the ring could be limited to as little as 50% in order to provide full redundancy for all of the users served by the ring (see Figure 5.7b).

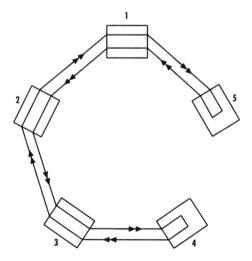

Figure 5.7b Path-switched SONET ring—with fiber cut.

Line-Switched Ring

The primary difference between the ring types is the manner in which
the fiber is used in actual operation. A line-switched ring can be either
two or four fibers (see Figures 5.8a and b).

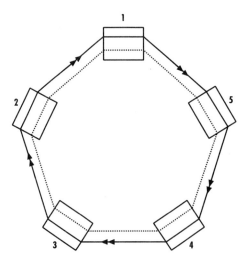

Figure 5.8a Line-switched rings (two fibers)—normal operation.

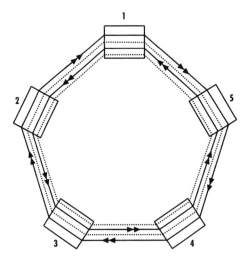

Figure 5.8b Line-switched rings (four fibers)—normal operation.

Traffic on the ring is sent in one direction during normal operation, with half of the single ring, one fiber, as the protection path. In the dual-ring, four-fiber implementation, traffic flows in one direction on one fiber of each ring, with the second fiber of each ring in idle standby. When a cable interruption, cut, or failure occurs, protective switching brings the second fiber of each ring into active status, completing the ring structure and maintaining service to all users (see Figures 5.9a and b). For line-switched rings smaller than 1200 kilometers, the restoral standard is 50 milliseconds or less. Due to the traffic pattern, a high percentage of the fiber's full transport capacity could be used in both normal and "cut" modes of operation.

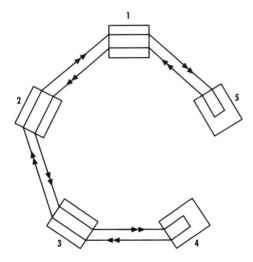

Figure 5.9a Line-switched rings (two fibers)—with fiber cut.

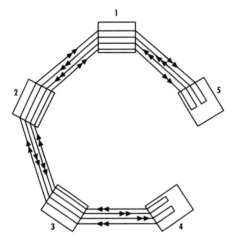

Figure 5.9b Line-switched rings (four fibers)—with fiber cut.

Frame Standard

Link quality is an important factor to the ATM network operational measurements. You will recall that link quality in another transfer mode was deemed less than desirable for ATM. In pre-SONET implementations, link overhead is sent in-band. The extent of Operations, Administration, Maintenance, and Provisioning (OAM&P) information is limited in scope and functionality. The SONET frame segregates the OAM&P data streams from the payload information and greatly expands the capabilities of the OAM&P functions. Providers are able to look at more discrete portions of the network and more precise inputs assist in identifying problems well before they escalate into serious performance degradation. When SONET is more fully implemented in the public network, the OAM&P information could be made available to users for traffic evaluation and performance measurements.

Frame Format

The Synchronous Transmission Signal-1 (STS-1) data stream, which is converted to an optical signal, has three elements in its frame structure (see Figure 5.10). The Synchronous Payload Envelope (SPE) includes capacity for information transport and path overhead. The Transport Overhead (TOH) is capacity reserved for the transport of status, messages and alarm indications for the preventive and reactive maintenance of the SONET links. Path Overhead (POH) is capacity in the SPE used to relay end-to-end OAM&P information between SONET terminals, on the same path as the payload information. POH and TOH information streams are important to ATM network users on a SONET ring because they provide source information for measurements of quality standards on a segment and an end-to-end basis.

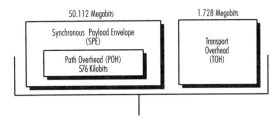

Figure 5.10 STS Frame Format.

Virtual Tributaries and Pointers

The SONET design allows for easy interpretation between SONET and current digital rates in service today. Through the use of a Virtual Tributary (VT), a lower-speed digital carrier signal is mapped into the SPE of the Synchronous Transmission Signal-1 (STS-1) for conversion to an optical signal. Virtual Tributaries are sized for the carrier stream it will transport, i.e., DS1 or E1 digital signals at 1.544 megabits and 2.048 megabits respectively (see Figure 5.11). The VT also enables SONET to pull a given signal out of the SPE without having to de-multiplex the higher-speed signal. The distinction between separate VTs is made with a *pointer*. Pointers identify the position of the payload in the STS frame (see Figure 5.12).

Tributary	Rate (Megabits)	Carrier Payload
VT 1.5	1.728	DS1
VT 2	2.304	E1
VT 3	3.456	DS1C
VT6	6.912	DS2

Figure 5.11 Virtual tributary chart, wideband services.

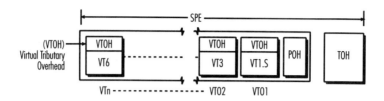

Figure 5.12 Synchronous transmission signal frame.

Within the synchronous digital hierarchy, a virtual container has similar functionality to the virtual tributary as described above with SONET. The pointer, though, in SDH only indicates the beginning of a virtual container.

Network Management Layers

SONET is a step above present carrier networks in the standardization of the overhead and the recovery response enabled by the monitoring of its remote elements. Built into SONET is the ability to recover from service degradation and link breakage situations without the need of human intervention.

The three layers of transport overhead—section, line, and path—are the network management tools which give SONET its distinction. Each layer corresponds to the path, line, or section segment of the network it represents. The three layers are separate from the information payload, but are part of the frame. Each layer protects the layer beneath and the accuracy and transmission of one layer assures the accuracy and transmission of the others.

SECTION LAYER

The section layer transports status data between the Section Terminating Equipment (STE). A section could be relatively short, representing the fiber cable between two signal regenerators (repeaters). This layer performs tasks such as framing, scrambling, transport, and protection of the line and path layers.

LINE LAYER

Communications between Line Terminating Equipment (LTE) is the function of the *line layer*. The LTE is, in part, responsible for originating and terminating the optical carrier level signal. The line layer provides synchronization, multiplexing, and error control to the payload, ensuring its successful transmission. This layer also performs the important automatic protective switching, based on preset thresholds. Capacity has been reserved in the line layer for possible additional functionality.

PATH LAYER

The *path layer* functions between the Path Terminating Equipment (PTE), which is responsible for multiplexing and demultiplexing the payload. The path layer performs the end-to-end functions of error checking, confirming source and destination of the payload, and identifies the payload's type, e.g., voice.

Digital Cross-Connect System

One of the important components of a SONET network is the Digital Cross-Connect System (DCS). DCS units have been extensively used in digital carrier networks, performing some of the same functions discussed here. The SONET DCS is either wideband, for speeds below DS3, or broadband, for DS3 speeds or higher. The primary function of the SONET DCS is to interconnect the fiber-optic rings. DCS is also critical to the effective deployment and use of SONET. The DCS supplies the optical carrier equipment with bundled traffic from many sources, and a common destination, to more fully use the operating capacity. Without the DCS, SONET would lose two distinct advantages, high utilization and an interface for European and North American digital network interconnection.

Add/Drop Multiplexer

The last component of SONET to be discussed here is also one that is unique to SONET (Figure 5.13). The Add/Drop Multiplexer (ADM), combines with the DCS to give SONET its physical self-healing capabilities, often detecting problems and rerouting traffic in advance of user inconvenience. The ADM functions like a pair of multiplexers, taking in many low-speed signals and one or more higher-speed data streams, with the added capability of selectively adding in a new input stream at an originating point, and dropping off data streams at their destination.

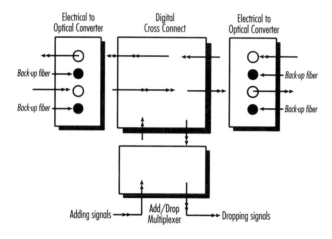

Figure 5.13 The SONET network.

The SONET and ATM Solution

Just as ATM is not a static standard, neither is SONET. Today trials and tests of SONET's flexibility and endurance are being conducted by individual network providers, and through cooperative ventures such as the Multi-dimensional Gigabit Information Consortium (MAGIC). On this SONET backbone, operating at OC-48 rates (2.4 Gigabits), the partners can bring together the collective thinking of many experienced engineers and scientists for the purposes of prototyping, product development, research initiatives into intelligent networks, network management, and emerging technologies. These partnering efforts and trials can only speed the implementation of SONET and SONET products more quickly. With ATM as the switching platform and SONET as the transport system an intelligent broadband network is in place and growing to support the increasing demands of the user.

ATM Switching

From the earliest days of telephony, a switch, or switch function, has been at the core of the technology. We have seen that a range of switch types have been employed for voice services, from manual up to the modern electronic digital switches, based on the Synchronous Transfer Mode (STM) principles. And not that long ago, packet switches entered the public network for data users. A Private Branch Exchange (PBX), also referred to as PABX (Automatic), and Data Switches have served as premises-based work horses over the years, giving many more users the opportunity to become familiar with the switching function.

Asynchronous transfer mode is, like circuit and packet modes, heavily reliant on the switching function to perform the unique tasks required of this new methodology. As we have seen, the circuit and packet switches, and even the premises-based switches for voice and data, cannot operate quickly enough, nor can they execute in the manner peculiar to ATM. Without question, the information rates specified for ATM, in the absence of any other requirement, far exceed the rates available on current switching systems.

Reviewing the principles of ATM we find that delay, fixed rate, variable rate, connection orientation, and connectionless orientation are several of the factors that have to be considered in the design of an ATM switch. The basic requirements specific to ATM could be summarized then (see Figure 5.14) in a few parameters that highlight the distinct characteristics of this new switch. These parameters would be similar to an ATM network switch and an ATM LAN switch. Of these terms, broadcast and multicast are not common switch terminology.

113

Requirement	Rationale
High Throughput	Support for Broadband Speeds
Low Delay	Time Transparency
Low Jitter Delay	Real-time Services
Broadcast/Multicast	One-to-Many Points
Low Bit Error Rate	Semantic Transparency
Low Cell Loss Rate	Semantic Transparency
Low Misinsertion Rate	Semantic Transparency
Low Blocking Rate	ATM Connection Orientation

Figure 5.14 Basic ATM requirements.

PERFORMANCE

In the ATM switch, performance is central to the manner in which a cell is handled within the switch, in terms of queuing and delay. Transmission of the ATM cell, originated in a variety of applications involving voice, data and video, does not permit a switching function optimized by only one traffic type. Therefore the queuing, movement, switching, and routing of the cell are fundamental elements that must be dimensioned properly, for example, to limit delay and jitter delay.

INFORMATION RATE

The issue of information rate is twofold, involving the switch speed and the application's data rate. The switch speed may eventually reach Gigabit speeds (an optical switch?) or function with parallel internal streams at lower rates. The data rates incoming from applications, ranging from low-speed telemetry to high-speed video signals, must be accorded the necessary treatment per cell for delay and loss ratios consistent with the parameters discussed earlier. This is a critical difference between current switches and an ATM switch.

One Point to Many

The integrated broadband network is intended to carry all types of traffic. Current networks and CPE products provide for sending information to multiple destinations. Whether this is accomplished today sequentially or simultaneously, the multi-point functionality is a desirable capability for an ATM switch. For both broadcast and multicast a "copy to" step would provide for all (broadcast) or selected (multicast) destinations. A copy function would also be useful in data backup and disaster recovery operations.

Switching Systems

Several switch types have been developed and actively tested in ATM networks. One or more of their names may be familiar from publication or through ATM provider presentations, such as Starlite, developed by AT&T researchers. Queuing is an important characteristic in describing a switch architecture. Three queuing solutions are possible: input, output, or central queuing. Each has different behavioral issues that affect the desired performance. The precise aim of the developers is to maximize switch efficiency, either by sharing buffers (i.e., central queuing), or by sharing several high-speed internal links across many lower-speed external links (i.e., output queuing). Commercially available switches may feature elements derived from each of the architectures, optimizing their product with the best mix of technologies. The switch in Figure 5.15 can be considered as typical of the models in existing ATM networks. Figure 5.16 lists the features of an ATM LAN switch. In this illustration, the selection of the switch type is for demonstration purposes only. Neither illustration is an endorsement of the product listed.

NEC ATM Switch Model #10	
Ports	48 T3 or 16 OC3
Connection Type	Permanent Virtual Circuit
Classes of Service	Variable Bit Rate (VBR) Continuous Bit Rate (CBR)
Buffer	Output
Switching	8 x 8 Matrix
Line Rate	311.04 Megabits
Throughput	2,488.32 Gigabits
Line Buffer	128 Cells
Port Buffer	4096 Cells per T3 Port

Figure 5.15 A typical ATM switch.

Forerunner ASX-1000 ATM LAN Backbone Switch	
Ports	96

LAN Modules	LAN Emulation
	100 Mbps
	155 Mbps
	    Multimode Fiber
	    Category 5 Cable
	622 Mbps

WAN Modeules	T1 (1.5 Mbps) E1 (2 Mbps) T3 (45 Mbps) E3 (34 Mbps) J2 (6 Mbps) OC3 (155 Mbps) OC12 (622 Mbps)
Buffer	Output (13, 312 Cell)
Throughput	Scaleable 2.5 to 10 Gigabits
Standards	ATM Forum Complaint

Figure 5.16 A typical ATM LAN switch.

ATM MULTIPLEXER

In the previous ATM figures, an ATM Multiplexer (ATM MUX) is shown as a unit external from the ATM switch. It may be co-located with the switch or remotely located to provide for aggregating many low-speed inputs on a high-speed link to the distant switch. During these early years of ATM deployment the ATM MUX will be an important network element for the provider to bring ATM network access closer to the user. With the increasing implementation of SONET rings, the requirement for the ATM MUX will wane as SONET takes on the responsibility for the user interface.

Figure 5.17 lists the access and support considerations which would be typical of most ATM MUXes available now and in the near future. Routing in the ATM MUX is based on the cell's Virtual Path Identifier (VPI) and Virtual Channel Identifier (VCI) fields of the header.

Ports	68 T1 34 T3 4 OC3
Connection Type	PVC
Classes of Service	CBR, VBR
Switching	Half Duplex Shared BUS
Line Rate	T1 ATM, T1 Circuit Emulation T1 FR/ATM, T3
Throughput	644 Gigabits

Figure 5.17 Conceptual ATM Multiplexer.

Summary

The more we see, hear, and read about any given product or service seems to make that product or service begin to come to life, to take on a character of its own. For many network users, getting through today, with what is in place, and keeping information flowing, occupies the vast majority of the workday. At this juncture ATM has been explained and the principles of the service are now commingled with the characteristics of the elements that comprise an ATM network. The actuality of an integrated broadband network, in place and available to nearly any user, is exciting to realize. Users can see into the mysterious network cloud and begin to grasp the significance of this new methodology and how ATM may fit into their own planning cycle.

It is important to feel this enthusiasm in order to commit yourself and your department's resources to studying and planning the migration of your organization into an ATM solution.

In the next several chapters we will look at the issues faced by users who have made the move into ATM. We will see what they have done and how they achieved their goals.

CHAPTER SIX

ATM Local Area Network

Introduction

In Chapter 4, the phrase "across the curb" referred to bringing ATM network speeds onto the user's premises, directly to the LAN switch interface. For many years, the high-speed LAN was restricted to an access arrangement that severely throttled back the operating speed of the LAN. Early LAN users were "LAN-Locked," not having any access to external resources. Primitive, contention-based, and deterministic user networks evolved into standardized methodologies, such as Ethernet at 10 Megabits and Token Ring at 4 and 16 Megabits. FDDI introduced a networking alternative that could cross the curb with 100-Megabit speeds; however, access was limited to direct-connected users.

Bridges and routers provided the speed and protocol conversions necessary to allow information from the specialized LAN onto other specialized networks. But the transition from the LAN to another network, e.g., the Public Switched Telephone Network (PSTN) dropped Megabit operating speeds into Kilobit transmissions. Improvements in bridges, routers, and hybrid "brouters" (bridge-router), in conjunction with changes in the type and variety of access links, provided substantial increases in transmission speeds for internetworking applications. The recent introduction of ATM technology in the off-premises network offers a leap ahead of the information rates found in traditional on-premises LANs. In this chapter we will look at how, through the application of ATM technology to the LAN environment, internetworking speeds in the LAN, MAN, and WAN are now equalized for the first time in history.

Developmental Activity

The ATM Forum, with more than 500 member organizations, is the focal point for the development and delivery of ATM standardized products. Its mission, to further the deployment of ATM products and services, includes Customer Premises Equipment (CPE), such as the ATM LAN hardware and software products. With the power and functionality of the workstation steadily increasing, it is desirable to accelerate information transfer for users, to improve the performance of current network applications, and to provide for more sophisticated multimedia applications integrating voice, data, and video. The ATM Forum, through its members, is rapidly deploying the only technology ever designed for local and wide area network use, to provide a high-speed information transfer platform.

Standards activity currently applied to the ATM LAN products includes the User Network Interface (UNI) for ATM network connectivity, Q.2931 for Switched Virtual Circuit (SVC) signaling, Internet Engineering Task Force (IETF) Request For Comment (RFC) documents 1483 and 1577 ("classical IP over ATM") for the transport of TCP/IP over ATM, LANE 1.0 for LAN Emulation, standards for congestion management, Interim Layer Management Interface (ILMI), Simplified Network Management Protocol (SNMP), and network Management Information Bases (MIBs). As expected during the early years of development, there are standardized and proprietary models, versions, and releases across the manufactured base. For example, Simple Protocol for ATM Network Signaling (SPANS), provides a robust Network Node Interface (NNI) signaling capability enabling advanced features such as IP multicasting.

The Product

The introduction of the ATM LAN switch, and the component hardware and software, is a major step toward significant change in the user environment. Products include a variety of switch sizes and devices for work groups, backbone connectivity, video and audio signals, management, and internetworking software. The systems currently in use are designed using the same technology employed in the ATM network which includes giving the user virtually unlimited bandwidth migration. Typical line speed, for a fiber-optic or Unshielded Twisted Pair (UTP) interface is 155 Megabits. The interface speed range on current switches is from 1.5 Megabits to 622 Megabits. As higher speed interfaces are developed, ATM LAN switches will expand their product to include the higher rate interfaces.

In Figure 6.1, switch characteristics are listed to demonstrate the services and features included in today's installed base. The ATM LAN switch is not a static, mature product. It is rapidly evolving and improving. New standards are being developed, such as UNI 4.0, which will impact the operational capabilities, resolve some of the proprietary methodologies in use, and add to the features lists of the products. Updated listings of services and features are available from vendors and network providers, who are also likely to share with prospective users their developmental plans and delivery schedules.

ATM LAN Switch	
Frame	Both Fixed and Modular with Multiple Slots
Number of Ports	Varies - Modular Cards 2-16 Ports per Card
Speed of Interface	155 Mps, Network T1/E1, J2, TAXI, DS3, OC12
Backbone and Desktop	Both, Classes of Service CBR, VBR, UBR, ABR
Media Interfaces	UTP Category 5, Multimode Fiber Singlemode Fiber
PVC	with VPI, VCI Routing
SVC	Yes
LAN Emulation	Ethernet, Token Ring, FDDI
IP Support	Yes, in some models with ARP Processor
Multi-Protocol Support	Proprietary and Standards Compliant
Buffering	Output Buffers - per Card and per Port
Network Management	Windows NT, HP OpenView, IBM NetView for AIX, SunOS/Solaris, SunNet Manager, and others

Figure 6.1 ATM LAN switch, services, and features.

The ATM LAN switch makes use of a Permanent Virtual Circuit (PVC) in the same manner as the network system. All switches have this base capability. The PVC is essentially a long-term connection established between two endpoints, giving the user consistent characteristics, such as class of service. The truly dynamic nature of ATM is realized with the greater flexibility of a Switched Virtual Circuit (SVC). The SVC is allocated to the user on demand, establishing a connection between the user and any end point desired, as long as resources are available and the end point is available to accept the connection. Set-up time is measured in milliseconds, and nonblocking architectures in the switch guarantee a path; but, as with a telephone call, the requested endpoint may be in use.

SVCs are featured by many switch manufacturers even though the signaling required for SVC operations is not yet standardized. Standard activity, however, is emerging, and manufacturers will move in that direction. One issue confounding signaling is that more than one methodology is under discussion. Manufacturers can currently choose among the UNI 3.0, UNI 3.1, or their own proprietary versions. Of particular interest are the potential capabilities that may find their way into the signaling standard. It seems more than logical to expect that the ATM signaling will eventually include typical "voice" features, such as call waiting, auto callback, etc. In the situation where the user asks for setup and the path is secured but the desired endpoint is in use, a call-waiting signal would permit that endpoint to ignore the request (return "busy" for now, but log the caller's identification, and schedule to call back when convenient), cancel the current operation and take the call, or put the first operation on hold, answer the call, and decide which to handle first.

ADAPTER CARDS

The selection of interface cards will vary depending on the selected manufacturer, the available adapters addressing a broad variety of connectivity. Typical selections include a range of bus architectures, protocol support, on-board cell processing, and media interfaces (see Figure 6.2). Most switches feature modular slots for the cards. The cards have from one to 16 ports per card.

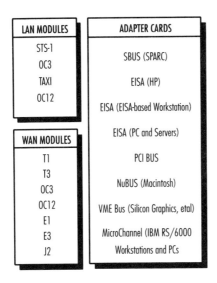

Figure 6.2 Adapter card selections.

AUDIO AND VIDEO

This product is used to transition high-quality audio and video from conventional video sources to an ATM network. The adapters utilize AAL 5, with some vendors offering multicast capabilities to ATM-networked PCs and workstations. Applications that stand to benefit from this kind of networking are medical imaging, security monitoring, distance learning, entertainment broadcasting, andpublishing/imaging databases.

INTERNETWORKING AND MANAGEMENT SOFTWARE

Internetworking includes the software suites for standards compliance, guaranteed performance, security, routing, configuration, and other attributes reducing network complexity. The software architectures offered are distributed multi-layered, as represented in Figure 6.3. Standards include AAL1, AAL3/4, and AAL5 for segmentation and reassembly, cell switching, traffic policing, MIBs, and classes of service for Continuous Bit Rate (CBR), Variable Bit Rate (VBR), Available Bit Rate (ABR) and Unspecified Bit Rate (UBR) traffic. The Physical Layer supports standards for the range of interfaces offered, including network interfaces such as T1, DS3, SONET/SDH, etc.

Figure 6.3 ATM LAN layered architecture.

Within the software suite, the user may expect to find the ATM Forum Interim Local Management Interface (ILMI) which provides device discovery and address administration for ATM-attached PCs, workstations, hosts, and switches. Network Node Interface (NNI) signaling gives the user routing and optimal route selection choices for automatic network configuration, simplified installation, and downstream management. Automatic service choices are permitted within the Applications Service layer, for example, to allow the option of selecting the appropriate Layer 1 network resource. Some models feature SVC use by upper layers for signaling to support private network node services such as connection management, i.e., admission control, call set-up, call knock-down.

Network management software is essential to provide administration and control for the user and the network through the use of tools such as network mapping, customization, monitoring of devices, links and services, traffic statistics, measurements for performance, and trouble notification. The SNMP-based management packages offer integration with several network management platforms and provide stand-alone applications for operating systems, such as Windows NT.

A Graphical User Interface (GUI) supports a range of platforms such as HP OpenView, SunOS/Solaris, HP-UX, and IBM NetView. Access can be via a serial port, an Ethernet port on the switch, or in-band on an ATM connection. SNMP trap notifications and records logging vary by manufacturer, with records maintained for log-ins, usage, traffic, and errors, etc., or sent to the management station for logging. The ATM LAN network management applications can provide for mapping of ATM- and conventional LAN-attached devices, a network component inventory, device-configurations, connection policy administration, connection auditing, and billing information.

Purpose

Manufacturers have been supplying ATM LAN switches for several years, acquiring experience and reputation for their products. Although the trade press has been on the fence, and on both sides of the fence, in their opinions of the success or future of ATM, the real success is measured by the user. Literally thousands of users have changed, or are migrating, to ATM technology with great success. Yet, some users are skeptical. This is understandable with new technology, because of the issues that are important to the users' organizations, such as investment risk. Established organizations are challenged by the intense, globally competitive marketplace and they are not anxious to risk their present information-technology investments on an unproven technology.

But the changing business environment is taxing existing networks with demands for more capacity and the introduction of applications which require massive quantities of bandwidth. New business starts are increasingly driven by information-dependent services powered by network-based applications such as interactive modeling, video conferencing, and collaborative computing. It is expected that manufacturers will build and market devices that target business requirements. As indicated above, because ATM technology is used to create a transparent network service for the transmission of all information, it is certain that ATM will be the strategic centerpiece for business internetworking. Vendors are aggressively pursuing opportunities based on backbone and workgroup (or both) marketing targets. Regardless of the sales orientation of the vendor, the user ATM switch provides functionality in four key areas.

Environment

The LAN, MAN, and WAN networks are provided with a high-performance, scalable networking service that adapts to user applications. Models are available for workgroups, backbone networks, campus, and enterprise implementations.

Infrastructure

Connection-oriented and connectionless services are combined into a unified switching infrastructure. The connection-oriented ATM switch is a fast, reliable, and dynamic connectivity vehicle for host computers, access devices, FDDI, Ethernet and token ring networks, servers, PCs, Macintosh, and UNIX workstations.

Applications

Existing applications, geared to the competitive nature of the user's environment, can transition directly to the ATM switching operation. These will then benefit from the improved capabilities of time and semantic transparencies, quality-of-service attributes, and deterministic responsiveness. New applications, such as networked medical imaging and distributed image analysis, requiring these same capabilities and generating a massive traffic load, will achieve optimal performance with ATM LAN switch's load independence. Direct user connectivity and connection-oriented resource allocation are useful in providing for cross-functional project teams associated with distributed applications in today's leaner organizational structures.

Investment

Recognizing the embedded investments in the user's environment, emulation, and adapter interfaces provide for transition to ATM internetworking connectivity without wholesale network changes. Existing single-mode fiber, multimode fiber, and Category 5 wiring are protected as well, with interface capabilities for all three media types.

Strategic Values

The ATM LAN switch overcomes one of the major limiting factors found in conventional LAN networks. The traditional solution of Ethernet, token ring, and FDDI is an architecture based on shared media and components such as hubs, routers, and bridges. With growth in user and application traffic, the typical approach is to begin improving performance by establishing router-based segmentation, which reduces contention in the resulting segments by lowering the number of users behind the router. On the surface this appears to be a good strategic move because additional investment is relatively low and workgroup bandwidth restoral is achieved.

But, what has actually been achieved? Look back to the Health Care environment in Chapter 3, User C. The situation and issues listed are typical of the busy, heavily loaded conventional network (Figure 6.4).Over time, growth in network activity increases the amount of traffic on the router-controlled backbone. Servers take on the additional burden of controlling traffic; server congestion, latency, and delay variations are increasing. Network predictability, maintenance, device placement, management, and control become primary issues for IS personnel.

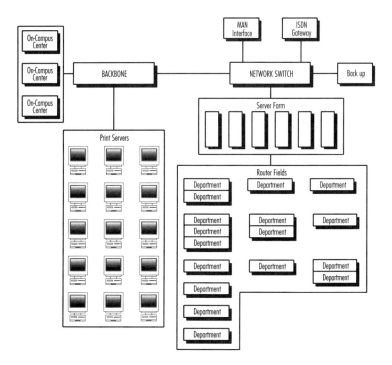

Figure 6.4 Typical segmented network diagram.

Although User C's situation did not include real time applications, the expected delay variations on the network would be unacceptable if, for example, video conferencing were a planned application. It seems apparent that some migration away from a network architecture that limits potential applications and poses a high degree of risk, is in the best tactical and strategic interests of a user's organization. Figure 6.5 shows the relative relationships that exist in a network with router-based segmentation. Particular attention should be given to the direct relationship between segment growth and Risk Factors.

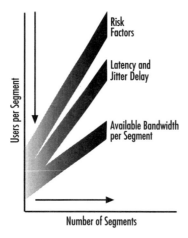

Figure 6.5 Segmentation issues.

Several alternative solutions may come to mind for resolving the apparent paradox in segmented networks. But, with such possible solutions as switched Ethernet, fast Ethernet, or FDDI, the organization may receive little value for its investment and may indeed be fostering a continuation of network complexity and limited functionality. Conversely, a switched ATM LAN architecture would provide greater value by its higher speed, dedicated user access, scalable information rates, guaranteed performance, operational simplicity, and LAN/WAN interoperability (Figure 6.6). These characteristics are most desirable for network-intensive applications. Furthermore, ATM technology introduces deterministic response, load independence, and an applications-transparent platform that provides for network traffic growth and the introduction of new applications.

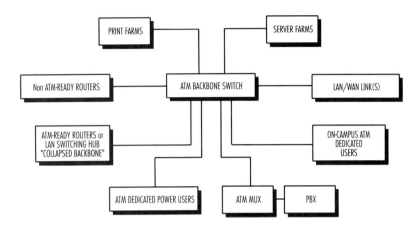

Figure 6.6 An ATM LAN switched network.

To better understand how the ATM solution is more beneficial, it will be helpful to look closer at the network architecture and the services provided to the user and their applications (Figure 6.7). Differences will be found between the methods in which the architecture is represented, and in how proprietary implementations enhance the services provided. This discussion will focus on the standards-based services that are generally available from all manufacturers.

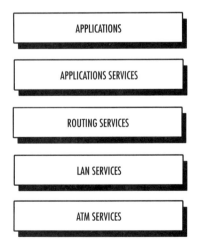

Figure 6.7 ATM LAN layered hierarchy.

LAYER 1, ATM SERVICES

The fundamental service in this layer provides the physical interface to the transport media for transition of the information stream into and out of the ATM network. Once transitional, at the boundary of the ATM network, all incoming traffic types are able to make use of the architecture's advanced capabilities (Figure 6.8). At call setup, the class of service determines the contract specifications for bandwidth, delay, and delay variations between the application and the network. Connection orientation guarantees transport capacity, but intelligent interlayer signaling gives Layer 1 optimization of the network resources by selecting connection types and link access most suitable for outgoing persistent or nonpersistent traffic, e.g., a short-length server inquiry message. Physical interface options permit direct connection of "power user" workstations and servers with demanding applications, and emulation access to users whose demands are less stringent. The media, in an ATM LAN switch, is the user's direct link to the resources of the network. No one shares that access, nor, because of the connection orientation, does anyone share the switch resources reserved for the user at connection setup. Bandwidth and quality of service are assured for the application. For servers, in particular, a direct connection eliminates the congestion on the backbone and the end-to-end switched connectivity greatly limits application contention for network access.

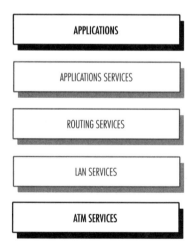

Figure 6.8 Layer 1, ATM services.

LAYER 2, LAN SERVICES

Because of direct connection interfaces, the ATM LAN switch could well become an automated wiring hub. The definition of LAN services in Layer 2 (see Figure 6.9), then, would not be dependent on the physical location of devices. Instead, networks could be designed based on logical designations, e.g., collaborative computing. This may not be so far-fetched: one manufacturer currently looks at this layer as a Virtual LAN (VLAN) service base. The logic in this product associates users within a common broadcast domain, regardless of the physical placement of the users' connections, e.g., LAN emulation or direct connect. Also, VLAN groups restrict broadcast and multicast messaging which increases bandwidth availability and provides "user segmentation" without network segmentation. Network resources are permitted to be multiple VLAN group members, supporting overlapping user responsibilities and resource sharing.

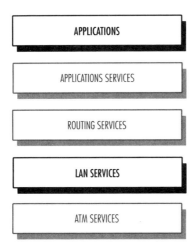

Figure 6.9 Layer 2, LAN services.

Layer 2 is where ATM Forum and IETF standards provide transparent services over ATM for applications based on protocols such as IP, IPX, and AppleTalk. Manufacturer implementations for configuration, scalability, security, reliability, and manageability are established in this layer.

Configuration includes identification and assignments based on LAN emulation, MAC addressing, protocol, departmental nomenclatures, application, or any combination of the allowable attributes. Identification attributes permit direct-connect devices to disconnect, move (roam), and reconnect at a new endpoint, resuming their former assignment once identification is verified.

Scalability refers to the distribution of services across the network, increasing capacity, and assigning users and resources to multiple switches and/or servers without degrading performance. Security, at this level, may be limited to authentication and authorization of user access to allowable domains, based on the vendor's implementation.

The highly reliable ATM LAN architecture utilizes distributed intelligence and redundant assignments of single logical resources across the network to provide a high degree of fault tolerance and the elimination of single points of failure.

Manageability is very much a vendor-dependent capability and the user must determine how well their implementation is accepted. It seems clear that configuration attributes such as "roaming" and logical domain assignments are useful tools that facilitate manageability. Other significant factors like management-software functionality, platforms and operating systems supported, and the usefulness of connectivity and display characteristics in combination with the vendor's software services give an overall picture of the total manageability of the system.

LAYER 3, ROUTING SERVICES

Implementations of routing services are based on a mixture of the vendor's experience and the incorporation of IETF and ATM Forum activity on Multicast Address Resolution Service (MARS) and MultiProtocol Over ATM (MPOA). MPOA is an ATM Forum work group, cooperating with IETF to standardize distributed routing in an ATM network.

Routing (Figure 6.10) is an essential service for device-to-device traffic, interdomain traffic, conversions between MAC types, and access to the global community. In current segmented networks, sizable investments in routers requires a transition strategy that is non-disruptive and protects that investment while phasing in the routing services of the more simplified ATM internetworking capability.

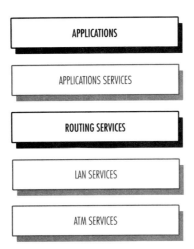

Figure 6.10 Layer 3, routing services.

Simplification is represented in the number of protocols supported across the backbone, and the extent to which domain assignments reduce routing requirements. Encapsulation capabilities are derived from the ATM Forum's Network Service Access Point (NSAP) addressing format. Where this is utilized by a vendor, a single integrated ATM network and network layer addressing scheme can be achieved. The two-part format allows a network-specific prefix, provided by the ATM switch, coupled to the device-specific network layer address provided by the device. This capability simplifies address administration and network troubleshooting. Also, distributed routing services would provide additional fault tolerance and a basis for internetwork link information for route calculations and route optimization.

Distributed routing service standards activity will produce a network-based Route Calculation Service (RCS) to provide what is referred to as "cut-through" routing for clients. A client is given the final route for SVC setup, directly to the destination, making the entire ATM network appear as a single network layer hop, regardless of the size of the network. [Note: This is similar to final routing procedures used in the public switched telephone network (PSTN)]. Distributed routing is currently implemented by vendors who recognize the constraints imposed in a router-based, segmented network.

With this implementation, the ATM network chooses the optimum route across the network, from origin to destination, and eliminates unnecessary delays and jitter delay from cell-to-packet conversions.

LAYER 4, APPLICATION SERVICES

Layer 4 is the interface for the applications entering the ATM network (Figure 6.11). Here, access control, bandwidth reservation, and *Virtual Channel* (VC) management activities are exercised according to the connection request. Usage records for auditing and billing purposes can be obtained at this layer as well. One vendor's approach leverages the application's "session-oriented view" of communications to establish a direct association between the application and connection, security, and quality services in the layer. For example, each connection setup request includes source and destination addresses and application type (e.g., Telnet, FTP) for that session. Security can be enforced based on a combination of ATM, Media Access Control (MAC), and network layer address, as well as by application, mapping each session to its own ATM connection.

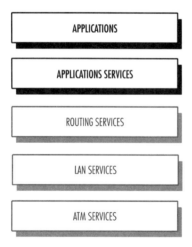

Figure 6.11 Layer 4, applications services.

One of the more significant features of ATM is its friendly approach to applications. Conceptually, ATM networks adapt to the application rather than the reverse (which is prevalent in conventional networks).

Layer 4 services, such as Quality Of Service (QOS) provide a guarantee on a per-application basis, whether that request is from an application optimized for ATM or a conventional application.

ATM Application Programming Interface (API) can be used to create ATM-optimized programs and to rewrite conventional programs to give them the same direct SVC control for their QOS, e.g., bandwidth allocation, delay, delay variation, on a per-application basis. With a well-tailored Layer 4 package, it is not necessary to rewrite programs since the network operator can establish policies to determine the proper services for a given application type. Layer 4 will also support LAN emulation traffic by mapping the connection request to the appropriate QOS.

Layer 4 services promote another important ATM design concept. That is to perform a task *once*, at the boundary of the network, rather than repeat the process inside the network. Using QOS as an example, Layer 4 is the boundary for the application entering an ATM network. The point of connection setup is where QOS is assigned, once, and it remains the same across the entire network. This systems approach is more beneficial than a router-based access scheme's packet-by-packet process because it eliminates the consequential introduction of additional per-packet delay.

VC management promotes optimization of overhead and network resources. Individual applications mapping provides for opportunities to select optimal routes for persistent traffic while making separate choices for "chatty" traffic. In systems which provide SVC capabilities, overhead can be controlled by tracking SVCs in use, allowing that SVC, when its parameters are appropriate for an application session, to be reused by that request, rather than establishing a new SVC.

Summary

Based on the concepts of ATM technology, it seems inevitable that ATM switched systems will become the core infrastructure in the user environment. The transition is made graceful by the introduction of emulation interfaces and integration with existing high-performance fiber and Category 5 media.

A transition strategy protects an organization's investment in current LAN technology in several ways, making the decision to implement ATM networking more palatable, even to the cost-conscious. By supporting existing LANs and applications transparently, equipment and personnel investments are secure, and training costs are minimized.

The result is an improved solution to today's performance challenges, a platform for absorbing growth, and the network capacity to introduce new bandwidth-hungry applications.

CHAPTER SEVEN

ATM Migration

Whoever said, "You can't steal second with your foot on first base," was probably not thinking about transition strategies and migration technologies. And in the development of the asynchronous transfer mode concept it may not have been clearly understood how this technology would be implemented. But the ATM Forum membership have a more practical approach. They know what we need, and they are aware that, for most users, there will be a need to keep one foot on first base while moving to second. That is the essence of an ATM migration strategy.

This chapter is oriented to methodologies that should prove useful in deciding how and when ATM technology can begin to play a role in your information systems. The introduction of this technology can begin in either the premises-based user environment or in the off-premises network linkages. In either situation, the migration process can be initiated independently of what is occurring in the other environment. The approach selected by your organization should target the area where ATM networking can have its greatest positive effect, and that migration could entail activities to integrate transitions in *both* areas.

To some degree, migration and transition have been discussed in previous chapters; however, the emphasis there was more *that it could be done*. Here, the focus is on how to do it, how others have done it, and suggestions for doing it yourselves. There is no doubt that for many users, a technological migration is not new, since there have been many such opportunities in voice, data, and video technology in the last 20 years. What seems to make this migration so different is that ATM technology is not specifically for any one information system; it directly affects every piece of information that is transported in the user environment and around the world.

Network Migration

Converting the existing telecommunications network to Asynchronous Transfer Mode will be a major undertaking. As indicated in earlier chapters, the construction of an ATM network will require the acquisition and placement of equipment, including switches, multiplexers, routers, and test equipment, plus redirecting the appropriate manpower for all the tasks from design and engineering to installation, sales, and operations. The process has begun, though, and for the last several years elements of the public and private networks have been migrating toward ATM. Initial test beds and commercially available implementations of ATM have been tailored to existing digital transmission systems, to ease the transition, and to protect the provider's investments in their networks. But, there is another purpose to this strategy, which is also directed at the user population.

Users have an investment in the public and private networks as well. These investments take many forms, such as existing commitments to equipment, facilities, manpower, and the applications connectivity requirements that serve our needs. With these things in mind, migration strategies have been developed, and are being introduced to users to demonstrate how we can transition to the future Integrated Broadband Communications Network (IBCN).

Network Services Internetworking

Specific migration strategies exist for most access services provided by the Interexchange Carriers (IXCs), such as T1, TCP/IP, Frame Relay, DS3, and OC3. Since these procedures are based on interface standards developed by the ATM Forum and other industry groups, such as the Frame Relay Forum, the standards are available to private network providers and the Local Exchange Carriers (LECs). As these providers begin introducing ATM connectivity, it is expected that they will provide similar migration plans.

The ability to mix and match ATM with conventional services will be essential to users in this emerging ATM environment until such time as ATM networks are more universally accessible. Although the IXCs currently have provisions to assist users in reaching ATM service points, these provisions are not necessarily aimed at the phased migration of existing access links.

The recent introduction of T1 ATM has established a networking platform that is appropriate for a much broader spectrum of users. T1 ATM is one of the most important migration efforts to come out of the ATM Forum because it promotes ATM service options for transport applications which serve the needs of thousands of small and medium-sized organizations. For this reason, the network migration concepts presented below begin with the integration of an existing service with a T1 ATM network link.

Frame Relay/ATM Migration

Frame Relay (FR) has become one of the most popular access services in the public network. A pseudo-packet switching methodology, FR introduced a more simplified transmission technique with greater throughput than traditional packet switching. It is a data-only service, but it fills a niche for DS0 and T1 level applications, that previously had few available options. For FR users with multiple locations, e.g., a multi-location college or business, FR/ATM internetworking allows a graceful transition to ATM networking while protecting existing investments and commitments in users' FR operations. Figure 7.1 represents a typical FR/ATM internetwork.

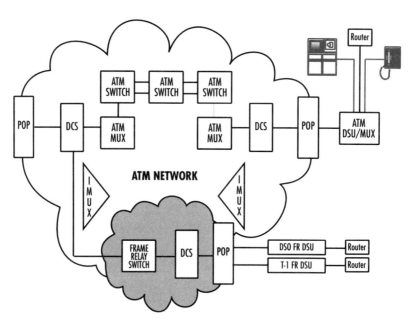

Figure 7.1 Frame Relay/ATM network diagram.

All FR/ATM implementations will follow the Frame Relay Forum's agreements for internetworking FRFs, such as FR/ATM PVC Service Implementation Agreement FRF.8, and subsequent FRFs as they are introduced. The agreement stipulates, in part, that FR-specific functions and ATM-specific functions be kept separate in the respective network elements. This defines the IXC gateway device, operating with AAL 5 in accordance with ITU I.363 BISDN ATM Adaptation Layer Specification. The network gateway device may be an ATM Multiplexer (ATM MUX), such as one described in Chapter 5. The ATM MUX's frame-side connection would be a T1 link to a FR switch, such as the Alcatel 1100 TPX. The ATM side is dependent on the IXC's implementation, e.g., T3. Inside the gateway, AAL 5 adapts the frame to cells, maps the frame's Data Link Control Identifier (DLCI) address to the appropriate ATM VPI/VCI address, and provides the upper-layer multiprotocol encapsulation translation. The encapsulation is for the Network Layer Protocol Identifier (NLPID), ISDNs Lower Layer Compatibility (LLC), or a LAN Logical Link Control (LLC) Sub-Network Access Protocol (SNAP).

In the ATM network, the Permanent Virtual Circuit (PVC) will be provisioned by the IXC for a class-of-service and information rate to meet the requirements of the user and the limits imposed by the ATM network implementation. Figure 7.2 is a sample PVC provisioning chart. The information has been supplied by an IXC service provider.

Provision		Frame PVC	ATM PVC
COS		Burst Express	VBR
Line Speed		64 Kilobits	64 Kilobits
Rate Policing			
	Bc	Zero	
	Be	64,000 bps	
	PCR		64,000 bps
Symmetry		✔	✔

Figure 7.2 Sample Frame Relay/ATM PVC arrangement.

The PVC provisioning is arranged in the FR and ATM network segments. In the ATM network the Variable Bit Rate (VBR) class of service is applicable. Policing of this rate is at Peak Cell Rate (PCR). The FR PVC is this IXC's burst express service with the information rate policed at excess burst. This allows the maximum burst rate to be at or below the speed of the access link, e.g., 64 Kilobits. FR and ATM PVCs must be symmetrical, meaning that the maximum information rate is identical on both sides of the gateway.

To the user, FR/ATM internetworking is transparent. Merging the two network types, in compliance with ITU-T I.555, FRF.8, and ITU-I.363, specifies the procedures to be followed to obtain the desired level of performance. ATM Adaptation Layer 5, initiated by the ATM Forum, provides many of the required gateway services. AAL 5 functions can be found in Chapter 4. Several functions are provided for in the ATM Adaptation Layer for the FR/ATM internetworking service. The primary functions include:

FR to ATM—Mapping the FR data link control identifier address to the ATM VPI/VCI addresses.

FR to ATM—The FR frame is mapped into the AAL 5 PDU; the frame's flags, inserted zero bits, and CRC-16 are stripped.

FR to ATM—The Q.922 DL Core frame header is removed and certain fields of the header are mapped into the ATM cell header fields. Message delineation and 32-bit CRC bit error detection are provided by AAL 5.

ATM to FR—Message delineation identifies frame boundaries and insertion of zero bits, CRC-16, and flags; protocol fields and functions of the PDU, received from the ATM user, are translated into the protocol fields and functions of the frame.

When configured for translation mode, the gateway will execute encapsulation mapping methods, NLPID/SNAP and LLC/SNAP respectively. The incoming AAL 5 CPCS-PDU and the FR Q.922 PDU must be examined in this mode to determine the type before overwriting the incoming header with the appropriate outgoing header.

When configured for transparent mode, the upper-layer multiprotocol encapsulation method is *transparent* to the gateway. In this arrangement the FR and ATM user equipment must support the same method, such as LLC/SNAP.

The ATM Location Transition

One or more of the sites in a user's network may be changed to an ATM location to support the FR/ATM internetworking. A typical frame relay site with 64-Kilobit or 1.5-Megabit FR links may use routers that encapsulate network layer datagrams into FR frames for transport. Router(s) connect to the network DSU/CSU via a V.35 interface, as in an IXC FR service, for example. When internetworking an ATM site with FR sites, the user must understand the software configurations of the CPE on the ATM side of the network in order to configure the FR/ATM PVC. The configuration will depend on the ATM equipment selected, whether it is supplied by the IXC, or if the user acquires provider-approved CPE. Routers support different IETF RFC upper-layer multiprotocol encapsulation methods, and more current router releases may be equipped with an ATM Interface Processor (AIP). The user's equipment provider, knowledgeable consultant, and/or the IXC will assist the user in determining the appropriate choices. Depending on the ATM service provider, current traffic, and planned traffic increases, there may be several options available to the user.

T1 ATM

Figure 7.3 is a configuration diagram for the T1 ATM transition. The existing router software, at the site, is upgraded to support ATM Data Exchange Interface (DXI) and the DSU/CSU is replaced with a T1 ATM DSU. Although the T1 can be provisioned by the IXC or the user, one strongly suggested principle in a migration strategy is to minimize the number of vendors/providers involved in the process.

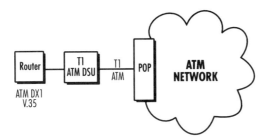

Figure 7.3 T1 ATM CPE.

T3 ATM

Figure 7.4 represents the configuration diagram for the T3 ATM transition. The existing router software is upgraded to support ATM DXI, the V.35 interface is upgraded to High Speed Serial Interface (HSSI), and the DSU/CSU is replaced with a T3 ATM DSU. The vendor-limiting principle for the T1 link, above, applies to the T3 link.

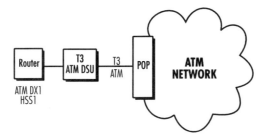

Figure 7.4 T3 ATM CPE.

143

For users currently equipped with certain routers, such as Cisco 7000 or 7010, there is an additional T3 option. The router can be upgraded with the ATM Interface Processor (AIP), eliminating the need for an external ATM/DSU (see Figure 7.5).

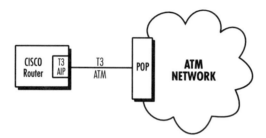

Figure 7.5 T3 ATM CPE with AIP.

Before looking more closely at CPE migration strategies, there is another option for the ATM network interface—that is, ATM connectivity extending into an ATM LAN switch. Figure 7.6 represents a T3 connection to an ATM switch, such as FORE Systems ASX200, Newbridge 36150, or GDC APEX. With this configuration the router/DSU arrangement is not required.

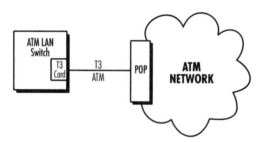

Figure 7.6 T3 ATM with ATM switch.

CPE Migration

Several years ago, tests were performed on Unshielded Twisted Pair (UTP) copper wire and it was determined that this medium would support transmission speeds of 155 Megabits. Many users were unruffled by this realization because their networks ran at 4, 10, or 16 Megabits. In most cases, networks are still operating at these speeds, or with fiber implementations; FDDI provides 100 Megabits to network users. Early in 1990, the first ATM adapters were shipped for workstations, and the transmission capacity of Category 5 wiring began to make sense. ATM technology, applied to the user's desktop connectivity, delivered UTP transmission speeds, and perhaps this interoperability with UTP assisted in forming the basis of a migration strategy for ATM networking directly to the user.

Category 5 wiring, along with several other components, is a common denominator in local area networks. Introducing a new technology to that environment would be difficult if the transition included massive changes to the major embedded elements of existing networks. Consequently, a strategy was devised to migrate PCs to ATM networking in a manner transparent to the user. To achieve this goal, it would be necessary to:

- Provide support for the widely used PC bus architectures.
- Provide support for the device drivers in the commonly used operating systems.
- Build ATM adapters and internetworking devices with LAN emulation capabilities.
- Utilize existing media, including UTP, single mode, and multi-mode fiber.
- Provide a network management capability for PCs.

This migration strategy is an outgrowth of the standards activities in the ATM Forum and the ongoing interaction between the Forum's member organizations, comprised of vendors, providers, and users. Because of this strategy, ATM networks are moving further into user environments, delivering seamless solutions to existing network problems and providing a high-performance transport capability for new desktop applications.

PC SUPPORT

The manufacturer's delivery of products that support popular operating systems and device drivers, shown in Figure 7.7, includes operating system and driver support from FORE Systems (as an example of the product availability in the market). Manufacturers, such as 3Com, UB, and other well-known industry providers, will have similar implementations. Availability of specific support products from each provider will vary based on their individual schedules and may be affected by the nature of their product focus, e.g., work-group vs. backbone connectivity.

NOS Support	Version
Novel Netware (ODI)	3.12, 4.1
Windows NT (NDIS)	3.5
Macintosh OS	System 7.0
Macintosh Open Transport	1.0

Driver	Environment	Adapter
Netware	INTEL X86	EISA BUS
Windows NT	INTEL X86	EISA BUS
Netware	INTEL X86	PCI BUS
Windows NT	INTEL X86	PCI BUS
Appletalk	Macintosh	NuBUS
MAC TCP	Macintosh	NuBUS
Open Transport	Macintosh	PCI BUS

Figure 7.7 FORE Systems PC support

EISA is widely used in the high-end platforms, with PCI gaining in popularity due to its promise of even greater performance. The PCI and NuBus support is essential to providing improved networking capabilities in the "sight and sound" applications used in Macintosh systems. This sample of initial support products should not be considered a final list. Each provider, such as those indicated above, has an extensive list of ATM products for a variety of networking requirements and computing platforms.

LAN EMULATION

An important step in the ATM migration strategy is the support of conventional LANs. With millions of PCs operating in bus and ring architectures, it is essential to promote connectivity without disrupting entrenched networks that represent sizable investments (Figure 7.8). Also, without a LAN interoperability approach, ATM services could not benefit existing applications which are resident on the LANs. Standards for emulation have been finalized and introduced, such as the ATM Forum's LANE 1.0 (LAN Emulation). Early implementations, based on a pre-standard version, are being upgraded, and it is expected that proprietary methods will migrate to the standard as well.

LAN emulation, depending on the pre-standard, standard, or proprietary version in use, provides for connectionless traffic in the ATM network, and encapsulation of ATM information in the higher-level SDU for point-to-point virtual circuits. The procedures that adhere to standards compliance, follow ATM Forum LANE 1.0, IETF RFC 1483, and Classical IP/MPOA (RFC 1577). Upgraded emulation capabilities have improved ATM functionality in the LAN environment. One such implementation allows the support of multiple, distinct, emulated LANs. Each performs as a separate entity, with respect to the other emulated LANs, and each has its own bus. This has a significant impact on broadcast traffic, which is then restricted to the devices on an individual emulated LAN.

Emulation services provide for internetworking between ATM, Ethernet, token ring, and FDDI LANs, allowing existing applications using Novell NetWare, Microsoft Windows, DECnet, TCP/IP, MacTCP, and AppleTalk to run unchanged over ATM Networks.

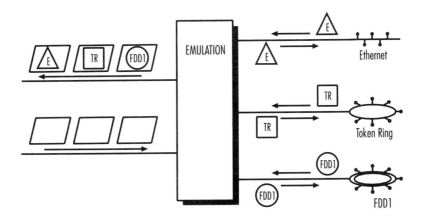

Figure 7.8 LAN emulation.

UTP SUPPORT

Over the past 20 years, fiber cable implementations in buildings and campus complexes has steadily increased. The high performance operating characteristics of this optical medium provide an acceptable transport infrastructure for migrating ATM technology into the user environment. However, Category 5 installations have predominated in the past and will continue for many years to come. Even though the cost of fiber to the desktop has become increasingly competitive, there are several factors which continue to favor the copper medium. Because UTP and fiber share the connectivity in popular networks, a complete migration strategy recognizes both types with individual ATM adapter cards. A common configuration shown in Figure 7.9, is copper to the desktop, fiber in the backbone riser.

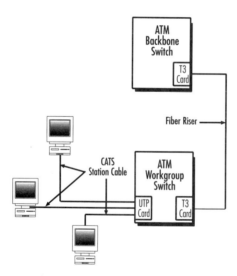

Figure 7.9 ATM UTP and fiber connectivity.

PC-BASED NETWORK MANAGEMENT

There are many UNIX-based network management platforms available for an array of computing operations, but it is uncommon to have a UNIX-based host in a native PC environment. One of the basic tenets of the desktop migration strategy is to introduce a PC-based network management system which is suited to this type environment. Most providers are offering only a UNIX-based system, however, it is possible to have a Windows NT-based package included in your ATM arrangement, from at least one provider. There may be other packages introduced, and more manufacturers may follow through on delivering a PC-based package. The user should understand, though, that a PC-based package may not make the fullest use of the provider's underlying management software. Most of the ATM management software available has been developed as an SNMP-based, graphical network package well suited to such systems as HP-UX, HP OpenView, or SunOS/Solaris. Be sure to have your provider give you a live demonstration of the management package you select.

Issues-Based Migration

There is a lot to be said for the investment-protection migration strategies listed above, but other factors may necessitate implementing newer technology. Several users have begun to migrate their systems into ATM networking based on performance, costs of present systems, and pressing business applications. In Chapter 3, the users listed demonstrate these and other factors. Regardless of the issues facing the user, an ATM solution is possible using a migration plan, which not only addresses the user's business need, but also provides for some level of investment protection for existing networks.

Many users will fall into similar categories, facing challenging issues that do not appear to have a solution in conventional computing and networking architectures. It will be helpful to look more closely at the issues the users in Chapter 3 were confronting, to project the scope of, and rationale behind ATM transitioning.

USER A ISSUES

"Before the overdraft requirement was introduced, the user was faced with an increasing volume of traffic, bringing with it a noticeable increase in response delay. More importantly, the issue became one of how to handle the current volume faster so as to minimize the cost implications of the new fee. However, with expectations for continued business growth, a second issue was to find capacity for that growth while maintaining the necessary time efficiency."

This user is faced with an increasing traffic load; plus, an external requirement is forcing the need to radically improve the time-sensitive nature of each tri-party trade. Routine system maintenance, not mentioned above, is usually a normal network function, but for this user, it was a time/cost-eroding process; for example, re-indexing the database, which is a 15-minute task. During such a period, response time is noticeably affected. The external requirement, the daylight overdraft, carried a daily cost of approximately $5,000.00 per day. That creates a lot of incentive to look at 15-minute re-indexing times, and to think about transitioning to an improved networking technology.

USER D ISSUES

"Interactive modeling and video conferencing, mentioned above, are good examples of applications which will become more commonplace in the work environment by the turn of the century. Because of the high bandwidth, low delay, and deterministic response time requirements, any of the typical LAN architectures would be challenged if these two applications were added to an already busy network."

Bandwidth-hungry new applications are the driving force—specifically, those applications which require deterministic response times and low delay. Conventional networking alternatives and router-based segmentation were considered, however, the performance levels and the lack of predictable response directed this user to new technology. A side benefit, just as with the user above, is that existing administrative users could continue to function in a LAN emulation mode, unaffected by, nor affecting the power users in the development centers.

USER E ISSUES

"In 1992, the federal government's High-Performance Computing and Communications program provided funding to increase the cooperative interaction between government and private industry. The purpose is to enhance competitiveness in networking technology and accelerate the pace of technological innovation. This mandate gives the impetus to structure new services to ensure the success of the program. New services would include distributed computing, interactive modeling, and cooperative applications software development. With each new service, transmission requirements and network flexibility, in the areas of changing traffic loads and the diversity of potential new interfaces, would be potential problems on the existing leased-circuit network."

The network supporting this user's connectivity, reaches into international locales from several of the 24 domestic locations. Traffic is using conventional leased lines, up to and including T3 service, but with growing traffic loads and new applications, such as collaborative programming, there is real concern as to whether the present links can continue providing the desired level of service. Performance, and perhaps some cost issues, was the catalyst to begin looking at different network methodologies. ATM cell-based traffic, by itself, would make a difference in the expected throughput on the T3 backbone[1] segments, and the network migration strategy would permit one or several selected locations to implement ATM, while the balance of the network remained unchanged.

USER F ISSUES

"The decision to migrate to a distributed network of powerful workstations is based principally on the concept of saving money. Introducing workstations on a distributed computing network would require a substantial transport capability to provide for interactivity and to provide for peak traffic loads. Also, current batch programs, would have to be modified to develop the interactive applications and graphical user interfaces."

Cost and a desire to implement interactive applications, which were not practical in a batch-oriented super-computer environment, provided the impetus to seek a networked solution. The business decision to reduce the "millions per year it cost to operate and maintain

---

[1]For example, consider a T3 backbone service utilizing switched multi-megabit data service at 34 Megabits vs. an ATM T3 backbone at 40.74 Megabits.

maintain" the present system was uppermost in their minds. Being at or near productivity maximums was an issue, but not an initial driver. The data files and load files were massive, and with 16 or more jobs running concurrently, any network solution would have to support impressive file transfers and allow the introduction of interactive applications.

Summary

If first base represents embedded networks, routers, and applications, then the stretch toward an ATM solution, at second base, is possible with "your foot on first." Network and premises-based migration planning appears to permit the broadest range of users to begin preparing for meetings with ATM providers. Learn what the IXCs, fiber providers, LECs and manufacturers have to offer. Listen to their migration strategies as they relate their proposals to your business issues. There is no crystal ball for a peek into the future, but if the explosive introduction of new ATM capabilities over the last year is any indication, within the next five years nearly every user, commercial and residential, will in some way be affected by the migration of networks and business systems to ATM solutions.

CHAPTER EIGHT

ATM Planning and Implementation

In many organizations there is still a fork in the organization chart which shows a split in the responsibilities for voice and data services. This fork may occur at the highest layers of the executive level. Furthermore, responsibilities for buildings and grounds (physical plant) and purchasing are often departmentalized in other, separate lines of organization.

Planning

Planning begins at the top with a business plan that clearly states the mission of the organization and states broad objectives to accomplish that mission. The plan becomes more specific at lower levels, where long- and short-term strategic plans are developed to guide the divisions or departments in meeting those objectives. Still further down, short-term tactical plans, project plans, and even job descriptions are used to give structure and guidance in meeting the top-down objectives, and delivering the bottom-up results.

With the emphasis on information today, a strategic plan for communications and computing is essential to plan the goals and objectives for information users spanning the entire organization.

And, according to their function, there are diverse computing and communications requirements. For several types of businesses, the recognition of the critical value of information and the thoroughness of the planning, has inspired a new title for the executive responsible for all communications and computing, that is the Chief Information Officer, or Chief Technology Officer. Regardless of the title, the job is to control the acquisition of information resources for all computing and communications, and to ensure that the information systems put in place are coordinated, at least functionally, to deliver the necessary results to satisfy the business mission. Before this type of organizational structure was adopted, departments exercised their autonomy by implementing disparate systems that may have met *their* objective, but could not communicate effectively, if at all, with the systems and computing resources elsewhere in the organization.

This chapter is a guide to planners, project leaders, team members, managers, and executives so that each might gain a deeper understanding of the intent and scope of information-systems planning and project management in general, and specifically as it relates to the strategic migration of ATM technology in the computing and communications systems environment. The information is primarily issue oriented, with some discussion of the acquisition process and project activities.

PURPOSE OF PLANNING

Clearly, the goal of any project is to reach a satisfactory conclusion. Depending on an organization's guidelines and performance measurements, this will include, at a minimum, meeting the project's objectives on time and within budget. In order to reach the project's goals, a planning phase provides the project organizers with an opportunity to thoroughly understand the scope of their project and identify every issue that must be addressed during its course. The issues can be grouped into four major categories:

1. Physical/Environmental
2. Logical

3. Operational
4. Financial

Financial issues are budgeting, costs, contracting, accounting, etc., which are organization-dependent procedures, tending to cover the same issues on each project, and will not be discussed here. The remaining three are germane to an ATM migration project and will be reviewed for that purpose.

MIGRATION PLANNING

The purpose of an ATM migration strategy is to provide investment protection for the hardware and software systems currently in operation. The purpose of migration planning is to minimize the disruption that normally accompanies a technology transition. The introduction of ATM technology allows the network manager to maximize the opportunities for higher-performance networking on the backbone, both public and private, give direct support to desktop users, provide LAN emulation interoperability, or begin with a combination of the three. The ultimate goal of the migration strategy, over some time period, is to build an ATM-based organizational internetwork.

The best way to ensure that the maximum results are achieved in the initial introduction of ATM, and in subsequent phases, is to spend as much time as possible in a planning mode, before the work starts. However, don't stop there. The old adage "plan your work, work your plan" does not leave room for the unexpected. By maintaining a planning mentality throughout the course of the project, the unexpected may still occur, but it is more frequently anticipated.

There are many PC and network-based project management applications that are useful in planning, executing, and tracking projects. They assist in establishing issue/tasks assignments and linkages where there are relational interactions in the project, e.g., dropped-ceiling grid and cable installation. The best place to start defining issues is in an orientation meeting with attendance from each of the departments/ divisions affected by the transition activity. The scope of the project will determine the extent to which each of the issues, discussed below, are weighted in importance and the effort required to reach resolution.

Physical/Environmental Issues

EQUIPMENT LIST

Figure 8.1 illustrates the issues that will be discussed in this section. The equipment that is to be acquired, and that will interconnect with the ATM products, is listed by department, location, ID, address, etc. The identification of all such items is essential to plan for their specific changes. Another entry on this list is the current interface specification for the device, e.g., UTP or fiber. The current interface may be changed as a result of the migration connectivity plans or the location of that device may change in the ATM network layout. Upgrades for routers and other Network components, such as V.35 to HSSI, or to the ATM Interface Processor (AIP), are also included on the equipment list. The interface requirements will need to be determined through contacts to the current vendor, or contacts to the prospective ATM provider. The new interface specifications for each item of equipment is another list entry, to assist the team in tracking the progress of changes and upgrades.

PHYSICAL/ENVIRONMENTAL ISSUES

Equipment Lists
Current Interface Specifications
New Interface Specifications
Space Evaluation
Power Requirements
Cable/Equipment Record and Inventory Plan
Move/Add/Change Plan
Network Type(s) and Technologies
Network Interconnections
Device Connection, Wire/Fiber
Communications Interface
Communications Interface
Management Interface

Figure 8.1 Physical/environmental planning issues.

SPACE EVALUATION

Space evaluation will vary based on multiple factors, such as construction and renovation, but the equipment rooms, rack space, shelf space for manuals, equipment placement, and desk space are critical issues that must be addressed. The ATM network elements selected for implementation, for example, may include a network management station that will be in addition to an existing management station. Desk or table space, floor space for an additional table, or for another rack, are possible unexpected necessities, and another entry in the equipment list.

POWER REQUIREMENTS

One of the most common unexpected situations that arises is power requirements and the associated connectivity. New devices will require a power outlet, perhaps dedicated, surge-protected, and with isolated ground. Normal operation, in association with a disaster prevention plan, may include a UPS unit, or having the outlet tied to a back-up electrical source, such as a generator. The electrical service arrangements in each organization differ, but the project should include time for determining the vendor requirements, verification of existing circuits, capacities, scheduling of any necessary electrical work, and recording more information on the list.

CABLE AND EQUIPMENT RECORDS

Cable and equipment records that are accurate and up-to-date are valuable source documents for equipment and technology changes. A per-location record of this type is especially important with ATM internetworking. If records are not current, or if they do not exist, this is an opportunity to make them current, or to establish a record. If testing of the cables has never been done, not been done for several years, or has not been recorded, it would be advisable to have the tests performed, at least on those cables involved in the transition. The test results, if maintained, establish a benchmark for downstream troubleshooting. The rest of the cables can be tested as they migrate to direct ATM connectivity. If there is no existing record, an inventory plan should be developed to gather all of the information necessary to

157

create the equipment and cable record. The immediate need is to identify the equipment and cabling that will be involved in the ATM transition the balance of the record can be completed as time permits. A record of this type is very useful for administration, maintenance, and MACs (moves, adds, and changes), and because of the introduction of ATM networking it should include, or be expanded to include, voice, data, video, telemetry, security, and all other communications and computing inventories. ATM connectivity will provide transport for all communications requirements, as you migrate further into the technology, and as additional ATM interfaces are made available.

MAC PLAN

A move/add/change (MAC) plan is a useful record for multiple reasons. No organization is static, and it is not possible, nor would it be practical, to impose a moratorium on moves, adds, or changes that may be made to equipment or facilities during the course of the transition. A MAC plan provides a means of tracking this type of activity to ensure that all devices and facilities are available at the time required for connection to the ATM network. An extension of this record can be used to track access requirements for locked or secure offices, resource areas, buildings, etc. MAC tracking will become more extensive as other communications systems are added to the ATM network. This expansion will require additional planning, not necessarily associated with the initial migration to ATM.

NETWORK TYPE

The network type(s) and topologies can be entered on the equipment list for quick reference, and to assist in planning LAN emulation implementations. Secondly, MAN and WAN sites may become involved in ATM network transitions. It is helpful to know whether the ATM network being offered is linear metallic, fiber, or an ATM/SONET ring.

For each network type, there is an interconnection migration plan or schedule that can be entered. An ATM work group may be followed 10 days later by an ATM backbone implementation. The initial ATM network implementation, although capable of integrating multiple accesses may, for example, phase in routers and/or premises-based ATM switching at later dates. Maintaining a record of the type, topology, and interconnection details, including actions required, actions completed, actions delayed, etc., will assist the team's control and administration effort.

DEVICE CONNECTION

ATM migration can be simplified by providing device connection, either UTP or fiber, to just those locations involved in the migration. The economies of scale derived in a total cabling project may not fit timing or budget considerations, and selective cabling is a possible solution. Be sure that all newly installed UTP and fiber is tested to meet the standards you have specified in your work order/contract. The test results become a part of the cable records.

Also, other devices to be connected in the ATM implementation, may require some change, e.g., V.35 cable length, or a cable to match a new interface, such as HSSI. The ATM vendor may supply interface cables, or specify what the user is to provide. This section of the plan is one place to record required connector pin assignments for new dedicated ATM adapter cables, e.g., the adapter cables for current LAN users may be reusable with minor pin changes.

COMMUNICATIONS INTERFACE

Voice communications systems, which will become involved in an ATM migration, will require details for the interface, any power considerations (such as for the ATM MUX), cables, location, floor space, and rack space. Ancillary information, such as traffic data, may be useful as well as having a voice person assigned to the project team, depending on the extent of the transition. As discussed above, integrating other communications information with data records will occur in an ATM network environment, regardless of the reporting structure of the organization and departmental responsibility.

The potential for including some video communications in an ATM implementation is very high. Video and/or sound-system interfaces become another tracking-record entry, and may require another team member. It bears repeating that the higher performance of ATM technology provides the capability to integrate existing video, in the initial *or* subsequent migration phases. This was not always the case with other networking technologies, and for that reason, voice, video, and data users will have to re-orient their network thinking toward the opportunities to integrate communications in an ATM network.

MANAGEMENT INTERFACE

The strongest networking methodologies are made more desirable with a network management capability to effectively administer and maintain operations. ATM switching systems offer a range of possible choices, some of which may integrate with your present systems. But when your ATM equipment selection includes a vendor-supplied package, the management and control interface requirements for that device becomes another record item. Other items, such as space, power, and cable requirements, are listed and tracked as well.

It would be nice to think that you are done now, but instead you should be getting your second wind for the uphill climb ahead. There are still more planning issues before the project work starts. The planning to this point has involved the equipment and its physical requirements. Next is the set of logical issues associated with the existing equipment that will remain in service and the new ATM equipment.

Logical Issues

ATM switching and LAN emulation is transparent to many network operating systems, but version dependent. Your existing system and network configurations will be the determining factors in the vendor's ability to minimize change and upgrades for all of the devices involved, from PCs to routers.

SOFTWARE LISTS

This grouping of issues (see Figure 8.2) is critical for vendor discussions and planning. The vendors will need to know what software is in use and what changes and upgrades are intended for the equipment and networks to be interconnected. Proper adapter cards, bus, driver, and router upgrades are device-dependent, as are the software version(s) in place. The range of adapter cards is also vendor-dependent, so the software list may be useful in helping to determine which vendor can provide the most thorough ATM implementation. It is a good idea to have a complete list of all systems, network, and applications software for reference, since the individual vendor will share any helpful experience they have had with the software on your list at other ATM implementations. Planning and project uses for these records are for tracking changes and upgrades that will occur during the transition phase(s).

LOGICAL ISSUES

Systems, Network, Applications Software

Management and Adminstrative Software

Diagnostic Software

Internetworking Software

Emulation/Mainframe Interface Software

Figure 8.2 Logical issues.

MANAGEMENT SOFTWARE

A listing of the management, administrative, and diagnostic software currently in use will also be of value in vendor discussions and planning. The current software set will influence decisions in the selection of options available from each vendor. There is a fairly broad range of choices, perhaps matching an existing platform. Planning functions will be dependent on the choices made for network management. The record for this issue is used to track the activities dealing with software; the physical issues are covered above.

INTERNETWORKING

The internetworking software suite and emulation packages are provided by the ATM vendor. The listing of existing internetworking software packages will assist the vendor in tailoring a proposal for your organization, and in specifying any changes that may be required for such items as mainframe access. A network migration, i.e., Frame Relay/ATM (Chapter 7), requires the specifications of the software configurations of the CPE for provisioning the PVC.

Maintaining software lists is a good practice for documenting licensing, versions, upgrades, and "fixes" installed. This same listing is a candidate for a new entry, *ATM optimized.*

Operational Issues

Each organization will determine the extent to which ATM migration will affect operations. However, the following issues would involve some changes that are of interest here. As you are going forward with the migration, by expanding the ATM network, operations changes will become more dramatic in areas such as disaster plans. This is due to the greater flexibility in the technology, emerging features, and potential implementation options. Perhaps the most profound change in operations will occur as the ATM network absorbs more of the communications transport responsibility.

OPERATIONS PLAN

There may be several names given to the document(s) which cover all aspects of computing and networking in an organization. Most of the issues listed in Figure 8.3 are a part of such documentation. The planning team members need to review these issues for changes in IS and all other departments and locations that are affected by the ATM migration. A dedicated workgroup, for example, would be given an awareness session regarding their change to ATM. This may include some changes in their procedures with regard to trouble reporting. It would not be nice to let a user think the improvements in performance and response are "imaginary."

```
┌─────────────────────────────────────┐
│  OPERATIONAL ISSUES                  │
│  ═══════════════════════════         │
│                                      │
│  Operations Plan                     │
│  Staffing Plan                       │
│  Staff Training Plan                 │
│  Trouble Reporting Plan              │
│  Disaster Recovery                   │
│  Disaster Prevention Plan            │
│  Management and Administration       │
│                                      │
└─────────────────────────────────────┘
```

Figure 8.3 Operational issues.

STAFF

In this time of downsizing, it would be imprudent to suppose that staffing plans will increase. The changes brought about with ATM networking may give rise to reorganizing reporting structures due to the integration capabilities introduced. The trend over the last several years has been toward combining communications and computing disciplines under one executive, the Chief Information Officer, and establishing that authority throughout the ranks of an organization. Specialists in all disciplines are still required because of the complex nature of each specialty. Cross-training will continue with pressures to streamline operations and existing staff should take every opportunity to increase their value through such training. The extent of training required with the introduction of ATM is related to the scope of the implementation phases, including the impact of network management options.

Vendor equipment and network implementations present different levels of commitment, ranging from familiarization sessions to documentation review and hands-on operation. But even these levels should be preceded with an opportunity to learn the fundamentals of ATM technology. Documentation and system prompts require a functional command of the technology, e.g., choosing set-up options.

Staff training will also include the people who operate the "help" desk. The vendors, manufacturers, and providers have support organizations established specifically for ATM assistance. Access to the support group is different than normal reporting numbers for most vendors. This will have an effect on trouble-reporting plans both internally and in the support groups. The help desk personnel will, over time, have a need to be more conversant with the technology to answer questions and respond to trouble reports. And, after all, even if it may not be nice, somebody has to be trained to say that "it's imaginary."

DISASTER

No one want to contemplate a disaster striking their organization, but unfortunately, it happens. Disaster recovery plans are a must in any organization, regardless of its size, whether the plan is written down or committed to memory. An industry has been built because of the concern for lost information and resources. ATM networking will prove to be a tremendous boost to secure, reliable information transport, as it is implemented on four fiber, physical ring SONET topologies. The greatest network transport protection will come when the metropolitan ATM/SONET implementations are in place. Then the self-healing ring structures are extended to the user on the "first mile" of transport. Also, the "copy" command feature, for multicast and broadcast applications, as mentioned in other chapters, is a feature that can allow direct copies of information to be automatically routed to on-site backup systems, and off-site disaster resources. The emergence of potential applications for disaster situations, addressable with ATM technology, is just beginning.

DISASTER-PREVENTION PLANNING

This is a hot issue. As the comedian Dennis Miller says, "I don't mean to get off on a rant here, but..." There is very little written or spoken word devoted exclusively to disaster-prevention planning. Many think this is part of a disaster recovery plan, but just the positive orientation of the word "prevention" should give this planning a much higher priority than what appears to be the case. Prevention is insurance *in advance of* the disaster. In the SONET situations mentioned in the preceding paragraph, there are single points of disaster, even with the metropolitan SONET ring. Most buildings are constructed with a single point of entrance for communications facilities that includes the buildings of the providers and most likely disaster recovery sites. Fiber for the SONET rings usually share that same entrance. Building riser chases are too frequently designed as a single chase. Multiple, or back-up, entrance facilities, risers, and equipment rooms incorporated in the initial design, or during some later remodeling activity, is prevention against disastrous events. The LEC's central office designs, including entrance facilities, for the most part may be the same as they have been for decades.

Pricing of, or costs for, alternate routes are high, running as much as the cost of the primary route and more. The user cannot effect changes with the carriers, but you do control your own environment. Figure 8.4 is a representation of disaster prevention opportunities. The back-up roof facility would not be required if:

1. your building has dual entrance facilities, and your ATM communications transport is via a physical ring topology, metropolitan ATM/SONET implementation, and if:
2. the metropolitan ring's other user interfaces and the provider have dual entrance facilities, and if:
3. the IXC or long-haul ATM/SONET ring has dual entrance facilities at each of its buildings.

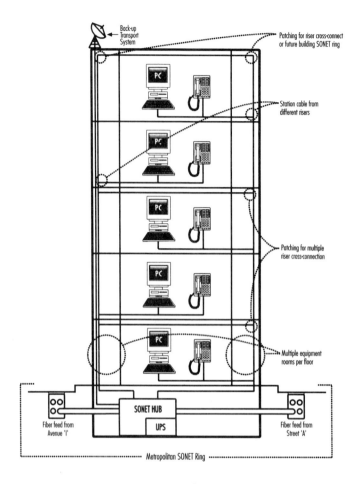

Back-up
Transport
System

Patching for riser cross-connect
or future building SONET ring

Station cable from
different risers

Patching for multiple
riser cross-connection

Multiple equipment
rooms per floor

SONET HUB

UPS

Fiber feed from
Avenue 'I'

Fiber feed from
Street 'A'

Metropolitan SONET Ring

Figure 8.4 Disaster-prevention plan.

Modern electronic switching, mesh networks, and SONET implementations have gone a long way toward improving network reliability and survivability. The marriage of ATM and SONET takes these past efforts to a higher level. The "copy" feature takes it higher still. End of "rant."

MANAGEMENT AND ADMINISTRATION

Over time, it will be possible to envision a simpler set of management and administrative functions when *the* network is ATM. Until that time, the transition of the organization's network transforms duties and responsibilities as ATM and other networks co-exist in some form. The transformation will be slight at first, and grow in complexity as the network transitions further, allowing the introduction of new applications and more powerful workstations. The simplicity of ATM does relieve network pressures, as the single technology, and its functionality replaces multiple-access arrangements and networking methodologies. The team will have to think through the management and administrative issues and plan for the changes that will occur, documenting and informing users as appropriate.

PROJECT ACTIVITIES

Once the planning is reduced to a mental state, and the project work starts, there are a few additional activity issues that are important to a successful ATM migration.

The assigned tasks will include a review of the organization's charts in order to identify power users and list "key person" interviews in the departments that are to be affected by the transition. Network administrators may be able to identify the busiest users, but within the department, the more productive power user may also be more efficient on network usage. Also, the selected vendor's system may provide for logical user domain assignments, which allow individuals from many different departments to share a virtual domain. Most managers would want to participate in assignment selections, leaving the IS staff free to focus on the technical issues.

TECHNOLOGY PLAN

For those organizations who have a technology plan, the technical activities become more focused by developing design statements for the ATM transition, based on the business objectives listed in the plan. For example, specific applications are used for meeting these objectives. The technology plan then can be useful in assisting the project team in developing an applications focus toward the ATM migration. And this focus is beneficial in discussions with vendors whose knowledge of the technology can be directed at an ATM implementation that is a solution to meet your business objectives. This, after all, is what you are trying to achieve.

SYSTEMS AND NETWORK MODELING

One of the most useful design activities is to prepare systems and network models to help describe functions and intent for the proposed transition. The models are useful in focusing on issues such as wire and fiber evaluation, vendor coordination, growth considerations, developing design statements, and identifying potential vendors. The responding vendors should likewise be returning their proposals with their model representations.

VENDOR SELECTION

Selection of the manufacturer and/or network provider and their products and services is only slightly different with ATM. Where possible, the number of vendors in a migration plan should be minimized, but the need for CPE and network components often leaves little choice. Primarily, there are only so many providers that have an ATM track record to look at today, and secondly, network providers and specific CPE vendors have developed strategic alliances to enhance their ability to meet your needs. These alliances can be translated into a good match between network and CPE entities. Where a strong alliance exists, the vendors have had an opportunity to define their respective roles, establish cooperative policies, and develop clear lines of distinction between their responsibilities. An alliance can be a major benefit and vendor alliance details should be considered essential in the vendor selection process. Obviously, the best alliance concept for the user is where one vendor becomes the single point of contact for all installed services and products. Procurement documents, Requests for Inquiry (RFI), and Request for Proposals (RFP) should request this arrangement and allow time for evaluation of the proposed response.

There are two other important specifications to include in the procurement document(s). These may be new to some users who have not included them in past implementations. For others, requesting these details is standard procedure. The specifications are testing of the installed system(s) and acceptance of system ownership. Vendors and providers are accustomed to requests, from prospective buyers, for their test and acceptance procedures, including some operational time period that is agreeable. The operating period will vary depending upon the installed system's size and complexity. Test procedures are commonly more precise. However, the user can request specific tests that are important to their business objectives. For example, a business objective could include the statement "For information to be useful, it has to be timely and accessible." This may translate into a design objective in terms of average response times and specific internetworking capabilities. This and other such design objectives then become the parameters for test and acceptance procedures. There should be a clear understanding with the vendors of what they can and cannot test, how they will test, and how they will define their results. All vendors are eager to showcase their ability to meet your stated objectives, and if necessary, work out any differences.

Summary

Anyone who has participated in an implementation project that had inadequate planning has learned, under fire, the purpose of planning. This process is critical and it cannot be adequately completed by one or more people without knowledge of the technology involved. Organizations will have to make time available to the person(s) who will be responsible for mapping out your migration strategy, planning the implementation, meeting with the vendors, and managing the project. Assistance is available from a mass of written material, knowledgeable consultants, associations, and conferences.

The technology is complex, but the operation of ATM networking is simple, and implementations are relatively easy to complete, if your designated personnel know how ATM works, the rationale behind its characteristics, and how it translates into an adaptable, applications-oriented, dynamic, high-performance, and integrated information transport system.

CHAPTER NINE

Conclusions

Side Issues

Literally hundreds of Local Exchange Carriers (LEC), Interexchange Carriers (IXC), and private network providers have invested billions of dollars in the telecommunications infrastructure, in this country and in the many nations of the world. The specialized networks embedded in that infrastructure provide each of us with the connectivity necessary for our work, leisure, security, news, and other information pursuits. Businesses invest these billions with the intent to make a return for their stockholders. Understandably, there is a vested interest in seeing that investment pay the anticipated dividends.

Some industry insiders think that ATM technology is not being implemented fast enough, that more should be happening. Because of their investments, it is understandable that not all providers are in a position to move with the same speed to implement a technology that displaces large portions of the embedded systems. Was that a reason, or more specifically were some of the industry's players holding their breath, awaiting the decision on the new Telecommunications Act? (see Figure 9.1). Well, the act has been passed and signed into law; it remains to be seen if the players in this brave new world will breathe new life into telecommunications or exhale some of the same stale wind since the AT&T divestiture.

Figure 9.1 The new telecommunications law.

ISDN

There has been considerable press regarding the LEC's inability to bring ISDN to the marketplace in an effective and efficient manner. (Did they have a migration strategy?) Some are even saying that they never learned how to sell that technology and that recent renewed efforts are a waste; the time for ISDN has passed. While the LECs are not universally known for innovation or the ability to respond to needs quickly, ISDN is an important product, especially in light of the goal to develop an Integrated Broadband Communications Network (IBCN). They must turn this around. Sell ISDN effectively, and introduce ATM, as well. Then there is reason to pay attention to the LECs.

But, first, why so much attention on ISDN, especially when the subject of this book is ATM? Simply put, ISDN is a basic building block of NISDN (Narrowband ISDN), and NISDN is a building block of BISDN (Broadband ISDN) (see Figure 9.2). ATM is the accepted set of principles being implemented to bring BISDN to reality. Consequently,

ISDN is a basic *migratable* element in the Integrated Broadband Communications Network and an affordable transition into the brave new world, even for residential applications.

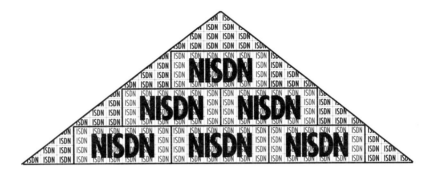

Figure 9.2 Broadband ISDN.

Telecommunications Reform

The Telecommunications Act has opened the doors to new competition that, in time, will present the user with a slightly different type of "option shock." Before the ink was dry at the signing, there were organizations on their way to the regulatory commissions with their filings for expanding communications services. There will be confusion, and it may be carried to extremes. In addition to the established communications companies, there will be ingenious schemes hatched. The technology is available for use by any entrepreneur, with many of the regulatory barriers lowered, to establish viable telecommunications business ventures in both local and long distance service. It is to our benefit that reform follows the introduction of ATM technology because, as we enter the new age, it is ATM which provides the methodology for users' and providers' interconnectivity and interoperability.

This new age is not unlike the pre-Bell System era in which literally thousands of providers competed for the telephony user. In those days there were technological and regulatory gaps that permitted telephone network isolation. It was common practice for business and residential users to have services from multiple providers in order to have access to separate areas of the same city, even to neighbors.

This is not the situation today. It is the providers who implement ATM technology that will have a distinct advantage over those who attempt to preserve or build conventional telecommunications access and delivery systems. Interoperability, integration, high-speed services, and transparent access are the keys to satisfying users' demands.

Through the use of ATM technology it will not be as important as to who provides connectivity. With ATM, it will not matter that thousands of providers are competing, selling out, or merging into one huge modern Ms. Bell.

Is reform needed? That is for someone else to decide. Is reform necessary to give users good service, reasonable price, and reliable access? Perhaps not, but with the widespread implementation of ATM technology users will have what they want and what they need. So much for telecommunications reform. The reformation issue here is the conversion to a universally accepted broadband technology. When that goal is achieved, then we will hear the "fat lady sing."

Historical Perspective

There were so many events that could have been included in the historic review—some just interesting, others nostalgic, but most of the major events and changes included were fuel for the explosions that created a telecommunications industry. The industry is now poised for change again, a change that will be beneficial to every user of telecommunications products and services in spite of the "Con-Sumer-Fusion" that will occur. One of the more significant changes occurring is Asynchronous Transfer Mode.

Over the last several years, a few courageous players recognized the need to speed the deployment of ATM technology. This sense of urgency led to the establishment of the ATM Forum. IXCs began deploying ATM systems to begin providing introductory network service implementations on T3 backbones. The ATM CPE is the result of both established manufacturers and new startups whose vision of the future totally embraces ATM technology. CPE, initially manufactured with proprietary and prestandards-compliant operating characteristics, is being upgraded to full standards compliance. The urgency is to meet the growing networking demand from new organizations with bandwidth-hungry applications and to meet the requirements of existing companies in need of performance boosts for their networks and applications. Alliances between the ATM CPE and ATM network providers has helped to increase the pace of network implementations, which have been primarily the domain of private networks and IXCs. But that won't be the case for long.

Local Exchange Carriers (LECs)

The United States has poked fun at the "seven dwarfs" created as a result of the AT&T divestiture. But, just as in the famous tale, all of these dwarfs have been busy in their mines (they are the major players in a $90 billion mother-lode), piecing together strategies for survival in the new telecommunications arena. The pundits have been waiting for the dwarfs to get ISDN off the ground, while the IXCs have been working with them to develop an LEC/ATM interface. The wait may be over, and the work appears to be bearing fruit. The dwarfs appear to be rolling out their ore trams loaded with gems of innovation and developmental work.

A recent announcement heralds the 128-Kilobit speed of ISDN for Internet access as being faster than a 28-Kilobit modem (see Figure 9.3). This is achieved with ISDN bonded channels, discussed in Chapter 1. Aside from the fact that several years ago, when users were struggling with the first 14.4-Kilobit modems, the same could have been said of basic ISDN access at 64 Kilobits, the announcement is an innovative gem directed at the needs of the user, providing high-speed transport to Internet servers and other destinations. If finally, several million ISDN lines are in use, there would be greater bandwidth and performance demands on the Internet servers and other locations. As traffic increases, the Internet servers will begin migrating toward a higher-performance technology. The clear option is an ATM solution.

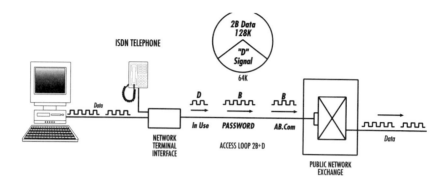

Figure 9.3 ISDN loop in bonded data application.

Another recent announcement is that one of the LECs will have ATM tariffs filed in each of its operating states by mid-1996. Other LECs are doing the same or will soon follow suit. With an ATM network in place, the LEC can achieve the IXC/LEC ATM interface, which, for all practical purposes, will foster more implementation opportunities, specifically in metropolitan networking.

Network

From the beginning of this book, the vast telecommunications networks of the world are presented as a patchwork of technological fabrics held together in part by the threads of standardization, put in place by the International Telecommunications Union (ITU). In its role as the global mediator of differing business cultures, applications focus, and economic muscle, ITU has formulated a series of recommendations to satisfy the differences with the introduction of the principles of ATM. These principles establish the technology, its operation, and how, through its application, ATM will bring to fruition an Integrated Broadband Communications Network.

The rationale behind that vision should be easier to see now, after looking at the variations in each of the network types in operation and developing an understanding of ATM technology. It is apparent that diverse network schemes cannot continue to prevail when an alternative method provides a higher-performance unifying methodology to address all the requirements that fostered the diversity. Fortunately, many of the IXCs, manufacturers, and private network providers that are responsible for the existing networks have been bringing ATM to the user (Figure 9.4). The momentum is increasing, and with the emergence of the LECs, it will continue to accelerate, bringing more segments of the network up to the new standards and introducing many exciting new applications to the commercial and residential environments.

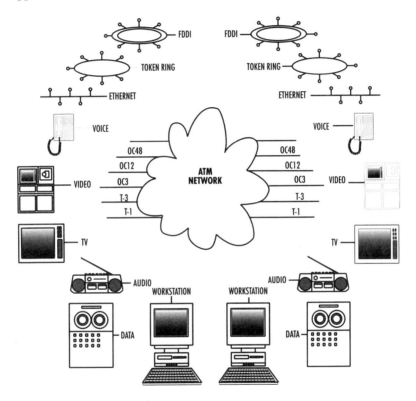

Figure 9.4 ATM networking.

There is still a tremendous amount of work to be done before ATM can be considered a universal network, available to all, performing in total conformance with the standards recommendations, and interconnected with hardware and software optimized for the technology. Availability is least problematic, because providers have plans that assist the commercial user in accessing ATM capabilities, including the migration strategies discussed in Chapter 7. Residential users will become involved in use of the technology simply through access to an upgraded ATM telecommunications network.

Compliance

From the information presented, *total compliance* can be inferred to include available transmission speeds that run the full range of rates discussed, e.g., from 1.5 Megabits to 5 Gigabits, more voice integration capabilities, and telemetry adapters. Also, many of the parameters, such as delay and delay variations, are projected on the basis of fiber-optic transport. The full extent of ATM will not be truly appreciated until ATM is implemented with fiber optic transport.

A natural fit is the deployment of ATM on SONET transmission systems. This technology marriage gives high performance on a highly reliable, fault-tolerant, self-healing transport platform (Figure 9.5). This is the ultimate implementation, yet it is disconcerting that so far only a handful of SONET rings are transporting ATM traffic. With SONET there is a reason for caution: Some IXCs have implemented SONET in a linear fashion, which means that the ring topology is logically established between two endpoints. Major fiber cuts that make the news, because of the disruption caused to users, are either fiber in conventional transmission systems or linear SONET implementations. An ATM user should know the SONET topology applicable to his or her ATM network.

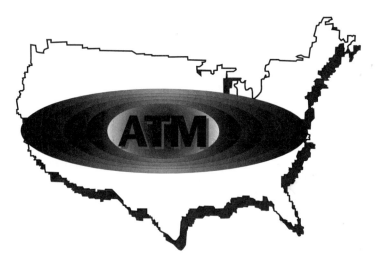

Figure 9.5 ATM/SONET network.

Hardware and Software

Ongoing standards and developmental activities in ATM technology are setting the stage for the introduction of new capabilities that are emerging and those still to surface.

Initial deployment of ATM networking used Private Virtual Circuits (PVC). Signaling issues are at the core of the more dynamic Switched Virtual Circuit (SVC). The SVC will replace the PVC implementations soon, now that the signaling standards are solidifying. The signaling protocols will give the user set-up control on a per-call basis and will provide for multicast and broadcast capabilities. Switches, equipped with a "copy me" feature will execute commands for broadcast and disaster prevention applications. Other hardware and software for interfaces, controls, congestion management, network management, and features, which will mimic voice capabilities, are sure to continue appearing on the surface of the basic ATM platform. As each new feature is evaluated, its potential selection will be dependent on improved or added performance.

Price

New technology is frequently introduced with proprietary pricing; ATM is no exception. Bottom-line dollars and cents frequently make or break technology decisions, but in an emerging market, price, derived from specific tailored implementations, is a considerable competitive advantage for the players and may in certain cases fluctuate between trial status and on-line use. The price elements include access, services, class of service, line speed, usage, gateway, and, if offered by the provider, network management charges. Monthly recurring charges (RC) and installation prices (nonrecurring charges, NRC) and Individual Case Basis (ICB) pricing are rated on a per hour, flat rate, and/or usage-sensitive basis. The listing in Figure 9.6 will be useful in understanding the cost factors that represent the price of ATM networking.

ELEMENTS	SERVICES	ICB	RC	NRC
Access	Local Link Central Office Connection Coordination			
ATM Port Connection	T1 T3 OC3			
Information Rate, per PVC				
Flat	VRB - 64K or 1M CBR - 64K or 1M			
Usage	VBR - 64K or 1M CBR - 63K or 1M			
Bulk Usage Received Cells	VBR CBR			
PVC	per end			
Gateway	Frame Relay TCP/IP			
Network Management	Fault Performance Access Link			

Figure 9.6 ATM price elements.

The price of an ATM implementation will usually be compared to the price associated with an existing or optional networking choice. The bottom-line price comparison yields an obvious result in real numbers, but it does not address the real differences that exist between the services. For example, compare a point-to-point T1 MAN link to T1 ATM service. Both services transport voice, data, and compressed video (Figure 9.7). The T1 link with TDM typically has reserved capacity for each voice line and may also reserve capacity for video, perhaps occupying half of the bandwidth, even when there are no calls or ongoing video conference in progress. With ATM, the switched service transports cells of information, on demand, whether they are voice, data, or video. Reservation is at call setup, based on parameters such as class of service and bandwidth. Plus, the ATM technology can allow the same T1 to be used for TCP/IP, Frame Relay, and ISDN traffic, perhaps eliminating the need for three other access lines and the associated equipment. The price comparison is imprecise; price alone has no factor for calculating higher performance and increased flexibility.

T1 TDM MAN	T1 ATM MAN

Fixed Bandwidth Allocation
Voice   6 Channels
Data   12 Channels
Video   6 Channels
	Dynamic Bandwidth Allocation
	PVC
	SVC
	     CBR
	     VBR
	Voice
	Video
	Telemetry
	Sound
	Security
	Frame Relay Gateway
	TCP/ICP Gateway
	Internet Access
	Network Management

	with ATM Switch
	PVC
	SVC
	     CBR
	     VBR
	     UBR
	     ABR
	Internetworking
	Workgroup
	Backbone
	LAN Emulation
	Virtual Domains
	Broadcast
	Multicast
	Disaster Prevention
	Disaster Recovery
	
	(list continued on next page...)

Figure 9.7 T1 MAN–T1 ATM/MAN comparison.

Commercial

Today commercial organizations are the primary beneficiaries of ATM technology because the development and delivery focus is directed squarely at their environment. Choices are available at the desktop to provide the transport capacity for power users, bandwidth-hungry applications, and a performance boost to existing applications. Backbone switches and LAN emulations provide a seamless high-performance internetworking service that also gives speed-matching interfaces to the ATM network service on the other side of the curb. Where business purpose and traffic volume warrant the need, a private ATM switch in the LAN, MAN, and WAN environments gives the commercial organization the flexibility to design a private network specifically tailored to its traffic needs, from the local desktop to the distant desktop (Figure 9.8). The range of potential applications is endless because of the utility of the technology in multiple environments and its adaptability to the requirements of individual applications.

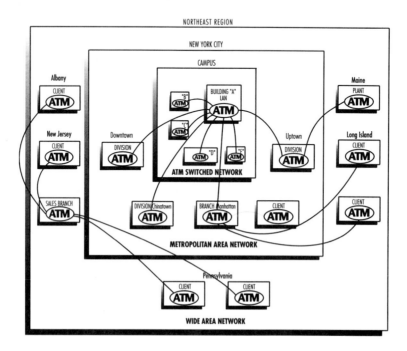

Figure 9.8 Private ATM network.

Residential

The residential arena may appear as a secondary beneficiary for now; however, the introduction of ATM by the LECs and the potential expansion in services from cable franchises will change that status. The question of who is the first or last to the marketplace with an offering is less important than the suite of services each vendor offers. ISDN is definitely an introductory service, giving one-upmanship to the creative LEC(s) presenting an effective campaign.

A multiple information ATM interface in the home will make the "smart house" concept more of a reality. It can be done now with a mix of POTS and electronic gadgetry. Drop the POTS and insert

ATM networking; drop the gadgetry, and insert UTP or fiber cabling, ATM switching, and ATM interfaces for the TV, security sensors, toaster, oven, lights, dishwasher, etc. Add a residential server with robotics and domestic engineering software, including telemetry for water, electric, and fossil fuels, reordering and bill paying, dietary and menu planning services, and there it is—an intelligent, self-sufficient, self-contained, policed environment that can feed the cat, walk the dog, and protect the youngsters from undesirable programming and information sources. And you don't need a key. Just don't forget your password and personal identification number.

Missing Pieces

A number of the items in the preceding paragraph have to be developed or incorporated in a cohesive, practical system. In actuality, few hardware or software products are optimized for the potential performance improvements provided by ATM technology. Licensing of the ATM Interface Processor (AIP) and similar implementations will allow more hardware to migrate to ATM connectivity. The ATM Applications Programming Interface (API) is a tool to assist in developing new and optimizing existing applications for the ATM environment. But the biggest obstacle will be to prepare the people and organizations for the blizzard of potential applications that are possible with this technology. There are users in the industry who are not yet familiar with ATM technology, let alone the mass of executive decision makers, who will be asked to sign off on ATM project plans and implementations.

Vision

The Information Age will be defined in terms of Before ATM (BATM) and After ATM (AATM). Telecommunications services and potential applications were hampered by inadequate line speed, delays, and low-performance networking. BATM users struggled to get information through bridges and routers where speed and protocol conversions consumed precious milliseconds per packet, where it then waits its turn for transmission on an access link operating at a fraction of the speed of the originating LAN. But in the year 2XXX AATM, the Chief Information Officer of the IBCN, in a desktop video conference broadcast to all 9.5 billion interconnected ATM power users, announces and simultaneously downloads to each user the newest feature upgrade.

It is not necessary to go that far to recognize the difference that ATM is making in real time. Desktop video conferencing (remember the Videophone?) is still not commonplace, and ATM networking is in its infancy. However, that has never stopped a visionary from seeing new possibilities in advance of technology's ability to deliver. Through ATM, technology is delivering today, and the communications bottlenecks and drawbacks will cease to exist. Boundaries and barriers that technology has been chipping at are now shattered.

A sight and sound ATM-optimized workstation will replace the PC, telephone, calculator, directories, datebook, fax machine, and so on. All communication is via one device. It is no longer necessary to wire the office for voice and data. An ATM switch/wiring hub's interface provides connectivity with an ATM-optimized Centrex using the same workstation link to your desktop. When you must leave your space, you disconnect your workstation, tuck it under your arm, and carry it along. At your destination, reconnecting the workstation to an ATM port activates an identity and verification process, establishes your user status, and accesses resources from that location.

With the ability to integrate all information types, a single fiber cable, four strands, will have the capacity to carry all the traffic from and to an organization. A one-inch entrance facility in two locations of the building boundary would permit different fiber ingress and egress points, establishing a disaster-prevention styled connection to the metropolitan ATM/SONET ring. Existing four- and five-inch conduits to the street could be sealed at the street end, allowing the rest of the space to be used as a wine rack for the information systems staff.

BATM regulatory constraints played a definite role in stifling the introduction of products and services in two ways. First, regulation itself kept potential players away from the table; they could not even touch the cards. Second, regulatory pricing policies both permitted and restricted innovation. The permission allowed long-term depreciation schedules with long-term capital recovery and a guaranteed rate of return. It's an odd combination for the players: they want to change, but their capital is tied up and there is little risk, so why change. The restriction was in the form of policies that required each product or service to stand on its own; cross-capitalization and cross-subsidization were not allowed. The same switching system that provides POTS provides ISDN, yet costs had to be allocated, separated, and pasteurized to develop unit prices that supported the service. It is no surprise that some LECs did not have a tariffed rate for ISDN for years. Reform will eventually affect this process. For now, ATM allows all visionaries an unbridled opportunity to whisk new products and services, at ever-increasing transmission speeds, to our homes and places of business. It just takes time and vision.

The Last Byte

Asynchronous Transfer Mode was developed as an outgrowth of the ITU's plan to implement an Integrated Broadband Communications Network (Figure 9.9). With ATM, a laundry list of new terms, definitions, and processes is rapidly becoming a part of our vernacular. In an effort to improve our collective technoslang, acronyms have been spelled out in each chapter with the intent to assist the reader with the new terminology of ATM, while learning about the complexity behind its development, and the simplicity of its operation.

Figure 9.9 The Integrated Broadband Communications Network.

Knowing what ATM is and where it can be used to make a difference in our work and leisure activities will further ATM's acceptance as a networking solution. Planning the role ATM will play and beginning the implementation of your selected migration strategy is the next step. Now we have come full circle, returning to a basic tenet of the ATM Forum: accelerate the deployment of Asynchronous Transfer Mode.

APPENDIX A

ITU Recommendations

G.703	Physical/Electrical Characteristics of Hierarchical Digital Interfaces
G.707	Synchronous Digital Hierarchical Bit Rates
I.113	Vocabulary of Terms for Broadband Aspects of ISDN
I.121	Broadband Aspects of ISDN
I.150	BISDN ATM Functional Characteristics
I.211	BISDN Service Aspects
I.311	BISDN General Network Aspects
I.321	BISDN Protocol Reference Model and Its Application
I.327	BISDN Network Functional Architecture
I.361	BISDN ATM Layer Specification
I.362	BISDN Adaptation Layer (AAL) Functional Description
I.363	BISDN Adaptation Layer (AAL) Specification
I.364	Support of Broadband Connectionless Data Service on BISDN
I.371	Traffic and Congestion Control in BISDN
I.413	BISDN User-Network Interface
I.414	Overview of Recommendations on Layer 1 for ISDN and BISDN Customer Accesses

I.430   Layer 1 Specification at the Basic Rate

I.431   Layer 1 Specification at the Primary Rate User Network Interface

I.432   BISDN User-Network Interface Physical Layer Specification

I.610   OAM Principles of BISDN Access

APPENDIX B

ATM Forum Specifications

- ATM User-Network Interface Specification Version 2.0
- ATM B-Inter-Carrier Interface Specification
- ATM DXI v1.0 Specification
- ATM DS1 PHY v1.0 Specification
- UTOPIA Specification, Level 1, Version 2.01
- UTOPIA Specification, Level 2, Version 1.0
- 25.6 Mb/s over Twisted Pair Cable Physical Interface Specification
- A Cell-Based Transmission Convergence Sublayer for Clear Channel Interfaces
- ATM 52 Mb/s Category 3 UTP
- ATM 155 Mb/s Category 5 UTP v1.0 Specification
- Introduction to ATM Forum Test Specifications v1.0
- PICS Proforma for the DS3 Physical Layer Interface v1.0 Specification
- PICS Proforma for the 100Mbps Multimode Fibre Physical Layer Interface v1.0 Specification

- PICS Proforma for the SONET STS-3c Physical Layer Interface v1.0 Specification
- PICS Proforma for the UNI 3.0 ATM Layer
- PICS Proforma for the DS1 Physical Layer Interface
- Interim Inter-Switch Signaling Protocol (IISP) v1.0 Specification
- 6312 Kbps UNI v1.0 Specification
- Customer Network Management (CNM) for ATM Public Network Service (M3 Specification)
- M4 Interface Requirements and Logical MIB
- CMIP Specification for the M4 Interface
- Circuit Emulation Service Interoperability Specification
- LAN Emulation Client Management Specification v1.0
- Frame-Based User-to-Network Interface (FUNI) Specification
- Interoperability Abstract Test Suite for the ATM Layer
- Interoperability Abstract Test Suite for the Physical Layer
- ATM B-ICI v1.1 Specification
- LAN Emulation over ATM v1.0 Specification
- ATM UNI v3.1 User Network Interface Specifications

GLOSSARY

This glossary is compiled to assist the novice and the seasoned veteran in becoming better acquainted with the technoslang of the Information Age, and as a quick reference list for the mastery of ATM terminology.

A

AAL ATM Adaptation Layer

AATM After ATM

access control Security protocol in the layered architecture that is connection-oriented and based on authentication parameters such as MAC address; or an application performed once at the network boundary

ADPCM Adaptive Differential Pulse Code Modulation

After ATM Conceptual terminology used to define the post-ATM era of the Information Age

AIP ATM Interface Processor

ANI Automatic Number Identification

ARQ Automatic Resend Request

asymmetrical A full-duplex provisioning parameter that allows different information rates for sending and receiving to co-exist on the same ATM channel

asynchronous A transmission, switching, or multiplexing operation that is not performed in relation to a time interval; unclocked

Asynchronous Transfer Mode A set of principles that defines a broadband switching and multiplexing information transmission system designed for use in the LAN, MAN, and WAN environments

ATM Asynchronous Transfer Mode

ATM Adaptation Layer The top layer in the ATM Protocol Reference Model, subdivided into the convergence sublayer (service-specific, i.e., CBR, VBR) and the segmentation and reassembly sublayer (payload PDU to cell/cell payload to PDU); supports the mapping between the ATM layer and the next higher layer; AAL 1, AAL 2, AAL 3/4, and AAL 5

ATM Digital Exchange Interface Protocol used over a v.35, RS449, and HSSI interface, e.g., router, or DSU/MUX for information transfer to the access link

ATM Forum Standards organization based in the United States with more than 500 members; its mission is to accelerate the deployment of the technology in ATM products and services for network and user environments

ATM Interface Processor Developed by Cisco Systems; replaces the DXI-equipped router and ATM/DSU combination; resides in a Cisco series router, providing a native ATM interface to the access link

ATM LAN switch ATM CPE switch, provides for workgroup and backbone connectivity for LAN emulation, ATM stations, and seamless internetworking with the ATM network

ATM migration strategy A user/vendor coordinated plan to transition ATM technology into conventional network services and/or user networks, i.e., LAN, MAN, and WAN

ATM/SONET The ideal fiber-optic transport arrangement for ATM cell-based traffic on a Synchronous Optical Network targeted by all providers

ATM/SONET ring Physical or logical topology of fiber optics and transmission equipment deployment

automated wiring hub Conceptual CPE vision for dynamic electronic "plug and play" patch panel; provides for logical domain assignment of users

B

bandwidth reservation Refers to the connection-oriented operation of ATM; with a request for transmission, the bandwidth needed by the request is allocated and held for the session based on Class of Service and other parameters assigned to the application; occurs during call setup

bandwidth-hungry A descriptive term for applications that require substantial transmission capacity; examples include desktop video conferencing, distributed image analysis, networked medical imaging, and video library video on demand

BATM Before ATM

Before ATM Conceptual terminology to describe the pre-ATM era of the Information Age

BOC Bell Operating Companies

broadband A bandwidth spectrum or transmission capacity of 45 million bits per second and higher

broadcast A network capability providing transmission from one point to all points on a network

C

Category 5 wiring Unshielded twisted pair station cable, 8 conductor, normally 24 gauge solid conductors; suitable for transmission speeds of 155 million bits per second over distances of 100 meters or less, manufactured to strict standards

CATV Community Antenna Television

CBR Constant Bit Rate

CCITT Consultative Committee for International Telephony and Telegraphy

Con-Sumer-Fusion Conceptual terminology to describe the suspected post-reform-era consumer confusion

congestion management The protocols and equipment attributes that combine to maintain throughput at all times including low-load and heavy traffic periods

connection-oriented mode A transmission methodology that requires an established path and destination before sending information

connectionless traffic Transmission onto a shared media or Ethernet bus, where capacity may exist and a destination may be available to receive

continuous bit rate traffic Describes information from isochronous, time sensitive, and continuous bit rate coding sources such as voice and interactive video conferencing devices, has highest Class of Service and priority, sensitive to delay and delay variations

copy to Also referred to as *copy command*, and *copy me*; a feature that provides one-point-to-many-point broadcast and multicast transmissions

CPE Customer Premises Equipment

CRC Cyclic Redundancy Check

CS Convergence Sublayer

CSTM Circuit Switched Transfer Mode

D

DD Depacketization Delay

delay The measurable difference between the time information is sent and the time information is received

deterministic response A predictable or known time delay for information transmission

disaster recovery plan A computing and communications guide for actions to restore operations in the event of one or more types of service interruption

disaster-prevention planning Positive actions to minimize one or more types of service interruptions

DS3 Digital Carrier System 3 (45 million bits per second)

DSU/CSU Digital Service Unit/Customer Service Unit

DSU/MUX Data Service Unit/Multiplexer

DXI Digital Exchange Interface

E

encapsulation Also called *multiprotocol encapsulation*, an inter-networking methodology for diverse network types, embedding datagrams in cells in one direction and the reverse process in the other direction

F

FCS Fast Circuit Switching

FD Fixed Delay

FDDI Fiber Distributed Data Interface

FPS Fast Packet Switching

FR Frame Relay

FRF Frame Relay Forum

FS Frame Switching

FTP File Transfer Protocol

G

gateway An ingress point for non-ATM traffic to enter an ATM network or an egress point for ATM traffic to transition to non-ATM traffic; for traffic conversion, i.e., *multiprotocol encapsulation*

GFC General Flow Control

Gigabit Billion bits per second

H

HDTV High Definition Television

Header Error Control The protocol in the cell header to correct single-bit errors and respond to burst errors

HEC Header Error Control

HSSI High Speed Serial Interface

I

IBCN Integrated Broadband Communications Network

IEEE Institute of Electrical and Electronics Engineers

IETF Internet Engineering Task Force

ILMI Interim Layer Management Interface

ILMI Interim Local Management Interface

IMUX Inverse Multiplexer

Integrated Broadband Communications Network Broadband networking concept of the International Telecommunications Union

Integrated Services Digital Network A circuit-switched service, a basic building block for integrated digital services, e.g., voice and data; two bearer channels at 64 Kilobits each and one data channel at 64 Kilobits

Interim Local Management Interface An ATM Forum protocol that provides automatic discovery and address administration for ATM-attached devices, e.g., workstations, hosts, and switches

International Telecommunications Union An organization with global membership; its purpose is to stimulate economic well being for all nations through the use of information technology; develops international standards recommendations

IP Internet Protocol

IS Information Systems

ISDN Integrated Services Digital Network

isochronous Descriptive terminology to define traffic that has a constant time relationship, e.g., ISDN at 64,000 bits per second is PCM coded at 8 bits per 125 microseconds

ITU International Telecommunications Union

ITU-T International Telecommunications Union-Telecommunications sector

IXC Interexchange Carrier

J

jitter delay Also referred to as *jitter*, the delay variations in transmission time for traffic composed of multiple segments, e.g., ATM cells.

L

LAN Local Area Network

LAN emulation A translation process to permit diverse network types to operate unchanged and to exchange information transparently

LANE Local Area Network Emulation

latency The time required to locate the first bit or character in a storage location, e.g., file server

LEC Local Exchange Carrier

LLC Logical Link Control, also called LAN

LLC Lower Layer Compatibility, also called ISDN

M

MAC Media Access Control

MAC Moves, Adds, Changes

MAN Metropolitan Area Network

Megabit Million bits per second

migration strategy *See* ATM migration strategy

misinsertion Cell loss due to bit error corruption of a legitimate address to another legitimate value; *misrouting error*

MODEM Modulation/Demodulation device

MRCS Multirate Circuit Switching

multicast A network capability providing transmission from one point to selected points on the network

multiprotocol Encapsulation *See* Encapsulation

N

Narrowband Integrated Services Digital Network A circuit-switched digital transmission service designed on the principles of Synchronous Transfer Mode; time division multiplexed time slots, minimum of 64 Kilobits, DS0 to DS3

narrowband Refers to a bandwidth spectrum or transmission capacity of 64,000 bits per second to 45,000,000 bits per second

natural bit rate A characteristic to describe an average information flow for a traffic type, such as voice, between a sender and receiver; maximums and minimums occur; the difference between the average and the maximum is known as the *burstiness* of that traffic type

Network Node Interface The point of connection for the access link in the ATM network

NISDN Narrowband Integrated Services Digital Network

NLPID Network Layer Protocol Identifier

NNI Network Node Interface

O

OAM Operations And Maintenance

OC Optical Carrier (i.e., OC48 2.5 gigabits)

OS/CLNP Open Systems Connection-Less Network Protocol

OSI Open Systems Interconnection

P

Payload Type Identifier A header field in the ATM cell to define the information contained in the cell, e.g., maintenance or normal traffic

PBX Private Branch Exchange

PCM Pulse Code Modulation

PCR Peak Cell Rate

PD Packetization Delay

PDH Plesiochronous Digital Hierarchy

PDU Protocol Data Units

Peak Cell Rate Defines the maximum allowable transmission rate per path or per channel; a policing mechanism to control resource abuse; PVC provisioning establishes a peak cell rate, which can be equal to the access line rate, i.e., Frame Relay (see Chapter 7)

Permanent Virtual Channel A logical connection established at service provisioning to provide transport bandwidth between points in the ATM network

Priority Identifier A header field that defines cell status for transmission decisions; Cbr Class Of Service has highest priority

PI Priority Identifier

PLCP Physical Layer Convergence Protocol

PLR Packet Loss Ratio

PM Physical Medium

POTS Plain Old Telephone Service

PRM Protocol Reference Model

protective switching Function performed in ATM switches to redirect traffic away from problematic routes

Protocol Reference Model A methodology used to depict a hierarchical layered architecture

PSDN Packet Switched Data Network

PSTM Packet Switched Transfer Mode

PSTN Public Switched Telephone Network

PTI Payload Type Identifier

Pulse Code Modulation A technique used to convert analog signals to a digital data stream; one sample every 125 microseconds generates an 8-bit reference of the analog signal values, e.g., *amplitude*, for accurate downstream demodulation

PVC Permanent Virtual Channel

Q

QD Queuing Delay

QOS Quality Of Service

Quality Of Service A vendor commitment to performance based on service parameter guidelines in the ATM Forum User Network Interface specifications

queuing Also known as *buffering*, primarily a function engineered into the ATM switch, a cell holding stage, before processing (*input queuing*), before and after processing (*central queuing*), after processing (*output queuing*)

R

RACE Research on Advanced Communications in Europe

real-time A descriptive term for an event or process that requires immediate response by the user or is controlled by the application, e.g., voice call or point-of-sale transaction

RFC Request For Comment

RFI Request For Inquiry

RFP Request For Proposal

S

SAR-PDU Segmentation And Reassembly-Protocol Data Unit

scalability The characteristic of graduated change; the expansion in performance and capability of the ATM switch

SCR Sustainable Cell Rate

SD Switching Delay

SDH Synchronous Digital Hierarchy

seamless Transparent interoperability with uniform quality, ATM internetworking, and LAN emulation

segmentation Function performed in the ATM Adaptation Layer, e.g., datagram payload divided into cell payload(s); (b)Design option in a LAN; divide users behind a router-based interconnection

self-healing A characteristic of SONET; automatic fault recognition and recovery without human intervention

semantic transparency A measure of the accuracy of information between what is sent and what is received, affected by bit errors, cell loss, and misinsertion

SNAP Sub-Network Access Protocol

SONET Synchronous Optical Network

STM Synchronous Transfer Mode

Sustainable Cell Rate A traffic management parameter defined in the ATM Forum's UNI specification for policing and/or contractual requirements, minimum allowable information rate

SVC Switched Virtual Circuit

Switched Virtual Channel A dynamically allocated transmission channel assigned at connection request setup, knocked down at completion of session

switching fabric Terminology used to describe an ATM switch, buffers, and processor(s); a switching system

symmetrical A full-duplex provisioning parameter requiring the same information rate for sending and receiving on an ATM channel

synchronous A transmission, switching, or multiplexing operation performed in relation to a time interval; clocked

Synchronous Optical Network A fiber-optic transmission system with a physical or logical ring topology, two or four fibers, and path-switched or line-switched

T

T1 Transmission carrier 1 (1.544 million bits per second)

T3 Transmission carrier 3 (45 million bits per second)

TASI Time Assignment by Speech Interpolation

TCM Time Compression Multiplexing

TCP/IP Transmission Control Protocol/Internet Protocol

TD Transmission Delay

TDM Time Division Multiplexed

Technoslang A conceptual term to describe acronyms

Telco Local telephone company

time transparency A measure of the sensitivity of information to transmission affected by delay and delay variations

U

UNI User Network Interface

User Network Interface An ATM Forum specification, the demarcation point for CPE and the ATM network

V

variable bit rate traffic Information from bursty, packet, and variable bit rate coding sources such as LANs and video devices; has a secondary Class of Service and priority, less sensitive to delay and delay variations

VCI Virtual Channel Identifier

Virtual Channel Identifier A cell header field that uniquely identifies a virtual channel routing through the ATM network; it from end-user to end-user

Virtual Path Identifier A cell header field that uniquely identifies a virtual path through the ATM network; it groups the end-to-end virtual channels

virtual A conceptual term to describe a software-defined entity or effect

VPI Virtual Path Identifier

W

WAN Wide Area Network

WORKS CONSULTED

Bell, T., et al., " Communications," *IEEE Spectrum*, January 1996, Vol. 33, No. 1, p. 30, New York, NY.

Braham, R., et al., " Consumer Electronics," *IEEE Spectrum*, January 1996, Vol. 33, No. 1, p. 46, New York, NY.

Cauley, L., "Baby Bells Rediscover Fast ISDN Service," *Wall Street Journal*, January 22, 1996, p. B8.

Chang, Y., Su, D., Vanderhorst, A., and Wakio, S., "An ATM Protocol for Local Access and Control of Internal/External Traffic," presented at IEEE Conference, Phoenix, AZ, 1995.

Charp, S., and Hines, I., "Telecommunications Fundamentals," *Bell Atlantic*, Philadelphia, PA, 1985.

Charp, S., and Hines, I., "The Basic Principles of Telecommunications," *T.H.E. Journal*, Vol. 15, No. 8, Information Synergy, Santa Ana, CA, 1988.

Engle, R., Bieri, T., and Keller, B., "Signaling in ATM Networks: Experience with an Object Oriented Solution," presented at IEEE Conference, Phoenix, AZ, 1995.

English, E., "TCP/IP Gets A Facelift," *Computer*, October 1995, Vol. 28, No. 10, p. 12, New York, NY.

Falcao, G., "Bringing the Intelligent Network to Rural America," *Rural Telecommunications*, September/October 1994.

Howe, C., "Synchronization in High Speed Telecommunications Networks," presented at IEEE Conference, Phoenix, AZ, 1995.

Hsu, M., and Chang, S., "A Method for Logic Design of ATM Adaptive Layer Protocol," presented at IEEE Conference, Phoenix, AZ, 1995.

Isaak, J., "Standards for the Information Infrastructure," *Computer*, January 1996, Vol. 29, No. 1, p. 185, New York, NY.

Knitl, W., "Asynchronous Transfer Mode in Broadband Networks," presented at IEEE Conference, Phoenix, AZ, 1995.

Krishnan, R., Silvester, J., and Ragavendra, C., "Jitter at an ATM Multiplexer in the Presence of Correlated Sources," presented at IEEE Conference, Phoenix, AZ, 1995.

Li, G., "Admission Control for Connectionless Traffic Across ATM Networks," presented at IEEE Conference, Phoenix, AZ, 1995.

Mier, E., and Smither, R., "ATM to the Desktop, " *Information Week*, September 25, 1995, CMP Publications, Manhasset, NY.

Minoli, D., Enterprise Networking: Fractional T-1 to Smelt, Frame Relay to BISDN, Norwood, MA: Artech House, 1993.

"Most Important Products of 1994," *Information Week*, December 19, 1994, CMP Publications, Manhasset, NY.

Negroponte, N., *Being Digital*, New York, NY: Knopf, 1995.

Perros, H., *Hi-Speed Communications Networks*, New York: Plenum Press, 1992.

Perry, T., et al., "HDTV and the New Digital Television," *IEEE Spectrum*, April 19, 1995, Vol. 32, No. 4, p. 34, New York, NY.

Prycker, M. de, *Asynchronous Transfer Mode: Solutions for Broadband ISDN*, second edition, Chichester, England: Ellis Horwood, 1993.

Rapaport, M., *Computer Mediated Communications*, New York: J. Wiley & Sons.

Readon, R., *Networks for the 1990's*, London, England: Online International, 1988.

Robb, R., et al., "Computer Aided Surgery Planning and Rehearsal at Mayo Clinic" *Computer*, January 1996, Vol. 29, No. 1, p. 39, New York, NY.

Sheu, T., "ATM LAN Interconnection with a Cut-Through Non-Blocking Switch," presented at IEEE Conference, Phoenix, AZ, 1995.

Siu, K., and Tzeng, H., "Adaptive Rate Control for ABR Service in ATM Networks," presented at IEEE Conference, Phoenix, AZ, 1995.

Tagle, P., and Sharma, N., "A High Performance Fault Tolerant Switching Network for BISDN," presented at IEEE Conference, Phoenix, AZ, 1995.

Venkataraman, R., "Designing SONET/ATM Layer Processing ASIC, Using Embedded Approach," presented at IEEE Conference, Phoenix, AZ, 1995.

Woo, T., "MPCBN: A High Performance ATM Switch," presented at IEEE Conference, Phoenix, AZ, 1995.

Wright, T., "A Case for Symmetrical Bandwidth," *Computer*, December 1995, Vol. 28, No. 12, New York, NY.

INDEX